Major endorsements for
The Power to Get In

"Absolutely anyone who needs access to important people needs *The Power to Get In* even more."

—William Beddor,
chairman, Japs-Olson Printing Corporation

"*The Power to Get In* will help a great many people open doors that would have otherwise remained closed to them. Boylan's Circle of Leverage is an amazing step-by-step system that will assist millions in achieving their goals in life. I found this book extremely stimulating and thought-provoking."

—Alan M. Miller,
CEO, A. M. Miller and Associates, Inc.

"Michael A. Boylan's Circle of Leverage System is a flexible but focused approach that can make the difference between getting the appointment you desire and getting turned away."

—Terry R. O'Neill,
president and CEO, The O'Neill Company,
board member and chairman, Association of Advanced Life
Underwriters (AALU), and former president,
The Twenty-Five Million Dollar International Forum

"All sales training is a waste if you can't get with the right people. *The Power to Get In* gives you the confidence and the competence to put aside all the natural call reluctance to get with the right people, time after time, because the tool set is so powerful."

—John A. Erickson
chairman and CEO, I. C. System, Inc.

"I like *The Power to Get In*, because it presents a methodical, skilled, sincere, and, most importantly, direct approach for cultivating prospects and new clients. Michael Boylan's plan is the edge you need in today's highly competitive environment."

—Roger Staubach,
chairman and CEO, The Staubach Company, NFL Hall of Fame quarterback

"Having access to the right people is an important ingredient in today's business world. You may be a talented person or have a super product, but lack of access will seriously limit progress. This can be changed with *The Power to Get In*. It is a proven process that works."

—F. James McDonald,
president (retired), General Motors Corporation

"If you want to gain a competitive market advantage, follow the strategies in this book to the letter. The soundest strategy I've seen since Ries and Trouts' 'Positioning: The Battle for Your Mind.' "

—Robert W. Pike, CSP,
president and CEO, Creative Training Techniques International, Inc.

THE
POWER
TO GET IN

MICHAEL A. BOYLAN

Foreword by
David McNally
Author of *Even Eagles Need a Push*

St. Martin's Press ✹ New York

9053158

Design by Richard Oriolo

Library of Congress Cataloging-in-Publication Data

Boylan, Michael A.
    The power to get in : using the Circle of Leverage system to get
    in anyone's door faster, more effectively, and with less expense   /
    by Michael A. Boylan. — 1st ed.
          p.   cm.
    ISBN 0-312-15193-4
    1. Interpersonal relations.   2. Direct selling.   3. Direct
marketing.   4. Job hunting.   5. Fund raising.   6. Persuasion
(Psychology)   I. Title.
HM132.B69   1997
650.1—dc20   96-32065
                                                                       CIP

First Edition: February 1997

10   9   8   7   6   5   4   3   2   1

CIRCLE OF LEVERAGE™

Contents

Section Three
The Circle of Leverage™ System:
The Ten Preparation Steps

Section Four
Making Your Move: The Five Execution Steps
of the Circle of Leverage™ System

Section Five
Advanced Moves

Section Six
Mastering the Circle of Leverage™ System

Some Opening Words of Comfort

Today there exists a great deal of abuse in the prospecting process. This abuse exists both in how people try to get in closed doors *and* in how their prospects keep them at bay. The sad result has been an ever-widening spiral in which everyone grows steadily more frustrated, angry, and difficult to deal with.

I believe this book will make the process of getting in the door more honest, direct, and comfortable for everyone.

My sincere hope is that through your use of the Circle of Leverage System, you will improve the quality of your life—by increasing your income, reducing your stress, adding to the fun you have in your work, and enhancing your personal life.

My goal is that the Circle of Leverage System will put some trust and respect back into the prospecting process and bring out the best in all of us, so that we are more courteous to one another and more respectful of each other's positions and responsibilities.

My dream is that the Circle of Leverage System will add harmony and reduce conflict wherever it is used.

As you read this book and begin using the Circle of Leverage System, please remember that the goal of the System is to create win-win situations for people on *both* sides of any door.

If you've already looked at the Table of Contents, you've seen that my step-by-step system includes ten Preparation Steps and five Execution Steps. That probably seems like a lot. In fact, you're probably thinking, "Fifteen steps! Are you crazy? No way do I have the time to do fifteen different steps for every person I want access to." I can empathize, because fifteen steps do sound a bit much.

But relax and take heart. The Circle of Leverage System is neither complicated nor demanding. In fact, if you use it correctly, it will actually *save* you a great deal of time, energy, money, and effort—while yielding much better results than whatever method of getting in the door you're currently using.

Imagine that you were being taught to set a table, but you'd never seen silverware, dishes, or napkins before. That simple task would be broken down into *at least* fifteen steps: covering the table with a table-cloth, putting out forks, putting out knives, putting out spoons, setting out water glasses, folding napkins, etc. But the actual process of setting a table is not difficult, complex, or time-consuming.

The same thing is true of the Circle of Leverage System. I've broken down the entire system into small, easy-to-digest pieces so that you can learn it quickly and easily—and so that you understand the psychological necessity behind each step. The process forces you to analyze, think through, and play out different scenarios, so that you can custom-create the strategy that is most likely to deliver the access you need and want.

Furthermore, once you've learned how the system works, it will *feel* like *only two* steps: preparation and execution. All of the smaller steps will run together into two natural, fluid sequences.

In addition, once you've gotten some experience using the Circle of Leverage System, you'll be able to whiz through all the Preparation Steps pretty quickly. In fact, if you want to gain access to many different people in the same industry or field, you'll be able to do the Preparation Steps for every one of those people *simultaneously*.

So please hang in with me as you learn my system and the principles behind it. It can save you hundreds, even thousands of hours of frustration—all for a small up-front investment of your very valuable time.

Enjoy!

—Michael A. Boylan

by David McNally

It has been said that the secret of a successful life is knowing when to change—when to replace what you've been doing or thinking with a wiser system, a more effective approach, or a better paradigm.

This book is about making such a change.

It's about approaching an age-old problem in a brand-new way, a way that's vastly more effective than anything that's been used in the past.

This book deals with the problem of *access*: How do we personally get to see potential customers, clients, or employers so that we can inform them about the product, service, skills, or ideas we have to offer?

Access has become an increasingly difficult and frustrating process. Those of us trying to get in others' doors—as well as those of us on the other side—have become more and more distrustful of one another. Business pressures have made us cantankerous and unfriendly, and very often we are operating on short fuses.

The people seeking access are tired and irritated. We're frustrated by having to make our presentations three or four times just to earn the right to meet with decision makers. When we genuinely have a great story to tell, we wonder why it's become so hard simply to set up a meeting.

The truth is that the people on the other side of the door aren't any happier. Experience has taught them to be suspicious of anyone they don't know. Many automatically assume that anyone who wants access will make false, inflated claims just to get in the door. And many of them are just plain tired of being pestered. The bottom line, therefore, is that no one's having any fun.

The problem is growing and now affects virtually all of us—business owners, managers, top executives, sales and marketing professionals, recent college graduates, and job transitioners. Furthermore, as you've probably discovered for yourself, the worse the problem gets, the less the traditional bottom-up approach seems to work. In fact, most of the time it doesn't work at all anymore.

I know from my own experience the challenges of access. I've lived, coped, and dealt with the problem all my adult life, first as a sales and marketing executive, and now as a business speaker and author. While I've managed to do well in the face of it, and am grateful for my success, I've long felt that if there was a way for me to get access to more influential people, I'd be even more successful.

That's why I'm so excited about *The Power to Get In* and the Circle of Leverage System.

The Circle of Leverage System is a genuinely new and highly effective way to open people's doors, especially doors that have been firmly shut. It is a step-by-step, top-down approach to gaining access that has been proven highly effective, over and over, in a wide variety of situations.

The system is utterly ethical, honest, and straightforward. It has nothing to do with smoke and mirrors, inflated promises, or slick sales pitches. And you can use the system in almost any situation—whether you're selling products or services, seeking job interviews, looking for corporate sponsorships for a charitable event, or trying to gain access to influential people for any other reason.

Furthermore, the system is simple to understand, remember, and use because it's based on common-sense psychology. It works by engaging people's key emotional drives and by making use of invisible leverage that already exists within the ranks of any organization or industry.

The person behind the Circle of Leverage System is businessman and author Michael Boylan. He's become a master at helping people get in their prospects' doors. He's developed his system over the past fifteen years, carefully testing, improving, and refining it. During those years—as a salesman, marketer, corporate vice president, and entrepreneur—he used the system to gain access to hundreds of important and influential people.

I would be doing Michael a disservice, however, if I said that he was born with a natural talent for getting in people's doors. He wasn't. It's the Circle of Leverage System that's largely responsible for his success, not some inborn personality trait. The System works—and sometimes works wonders—precisely because it is adaptable to a wide range of people, personality types, situations, and sizes of companies.

Best of all, though, the Circle of Leverage System provides a win-win strategy for everyone—both the person seeking access and the person they hope to reach—by saving everyone time, eliminating drudgery, and promoting honesty and straightforwardness across the board. And that makes me especially enthusiastic about Michael Boylan's leading-edge system.

Each of us has two choices in how to deal with the problem of access: We can do nothing and stay trapped in a downward spiral of frustration and failure, or we can take a new, different, and vastly more effective approach.

The Circle of Leverage System is that approach—one that will make things better for you *and* the people you wish to access. At the same time, it will make the environment in which we all have to work a better place for us all.

If you're ready to learn to soar through people's doors, turn the page.

How This Book Was Born

In 1990, at the age of thirty, I owned and ran two successful companies. I was having fun. Things were good.

But around this time, my strong-minded grandmother, Elinor, began to vocalize her disappointment with me. She knew I was not pursuing my childhood dream, which was to become a successful singer/songwriter. She began to challenge me: "Michael, you'll be eighty years old someday. Your grandchildren will be gathered around you, and I'll be listening from heaven as you say to them, 'You know, kids, I could have been a famous singer.' And I'll hear them say back, 'Well, why weren't you? How come you didn't try it?' "

At first I tried to ignore her—after all, I had two companies, employees, and customers to take care of. But she persisted. I couldn't hide from her constant questioning, and eventually her words sank in.

So, with the goal of being signed by a major record label, I put together a plan to break into the recording industry. I knew it wouldn't be easy. Some of my mentors, business advisers, and trusted friends warned me: "Michael, you've targeted one of the toughest businesses on earth. Your chances for success are terrible. You're one out of about ten thousand people who approach the major labels *every month*, hoping to get a recording contract. The executives in the industry are simply not going to pay attention to you. Plus, you have no story, no track record! You don't have a prayer of getting in their doors."

In response, I said, "Thanks for your advice. But I'm pretty good at getting into people's doors. Just watch."

Over the next twelve months I recorded more than ten songs. I wanted my demo product to be the best it could be, so I spared no expense and hired top-notch musicians who had played with Prince, Bruce Hornsby, Steve Miller, Michael Bolton, the Minnesota Orchestra, and the Los Angeles Philharmonic. I also produced a video to accompany my CD and cassette.

Finally, in the fall of 1991, everything was ready. I began my quest to gain direct access to the biggest movers and shakers in the music industry, using a strategy I'd put together from my years as an entrepreneur.

In the months that followed, two very unexpected things happened.

Number one: Even though I was a total unknown—I had no track record, no connections, no referrals, and no famous name to cash in on—I succeeded in gaining access to key executives at *all* of the major labels and most of the key independents. In fact, I created quite a buzz in the recording industry among these people, because they couldn't figure out how I had managed to get in their doors. Some even started calling each other to talk about me and how I had managed to gain access to them.

Number two: I didn't get a recording contract. Though plenty of people opened their doors to me, none were interested in my music. To say I was very disappointed is putting it mildly.

What finally helped open my eyes was a conversation I had with the CEO and President of one of the largest recording companies in the world:

Me: Mr._____, thank you for taking the call. Can I speak for one minute? I'm calling to find out if you've listened to my songs, and if you're interested in them.

CEO: No, Michael, they're not Top Ten material. I don't think they'll fly. Now, who are you? Do you have some kind of band there in Minnesota?

Me: No, sir.

CEO: Are you playing anywhere now?

Me: No, sir.

CEO: Do you have any kind of following at all?

Me: No, sir.

CEO: I see. Are you looking for a job?

Me: No, sir, I'm just trying to learn what I can do to the songs so I can land a recording contract.

CEO: Michael, I don't think you're listening. . . . Now, is it true that you also spoke with _____ (President of another major label) about one month ago?

Me: Yes, sir.

CEO: I've heard that you also got to_____(Senior Vice President of another very large label).

Me: Yes, sir.

CEO: I guess you've also talked with_____,_____, and_____(top executives at three other big labels). Is that correct?

Me: Yes, sir, it is.

CEO: Michael, how in the hell are you doing all this?

Me: Well, sir, I'm pretty good at getting in the door.

CEO: Well, that's obvious! I can see that! Do you know how many unsolicited cassettes we get from people like you? About ten thousand, sometimes fifteen thousand a month. Think I have time to pay any attention to many of these people?

Me: No, sir, I'm sure you don't.

CEO: Well, I think it's amazing that you've caused me to want to pay attention to you, without any track record or credibility in our business. I admire your talent at getting in the door. In fact, we could use it here. I'm not interested in your music, Michael, but I *am* interested in having you train our sales force in whatever it is that you do.

Me: Thank you, sir, but I don't really know what I'd teach. Over the years, I've just become very good at getting in.

CEO: My advice to you, Michael, is that I'd get out of the music business if I were you. I'd write a book about whatever it is that you're doing to get into people's doors. I'd share that talent with everyone else. It's extremely valuable, and needed. Good-bye.

After hearing this sort of response over and over from executive after executive, the message sank in. So I changed my focus, put my music aside, and in late 1993, began to use my get-in-the-door skills to earn a living.

I took a job as Vice President of Sales for a privately held company that sold document processing and imaging services to Fortune 500 firms involved in document-intensive litigation. It was here that I fine-tuned and packaged my system, and proved how effective and valuable it could be for others.

During this period, I put the power of my system to work five days a week. And in the evenings and on weekends I wrote this book.

My employer's most prized prospects were the general counsels (top lawyers) of Fortune 500 companies. These people are notoriously difficult to see. Before I joined the company, my employer's salespeople were rarely able to book appointments with these general counsels. They'd usually have to settle for a low-level lawyer in the litigation department, or even a senior paralegal; then they'd have to slowly and gradually work their way up, step by step, hoping to get heard by the people who had the power to purchase my company's services.

I changed all that. In four months, using my system—which by now I'd named the Circle of Leverage—I delivered thirty-minute face-to-face appointments with the general counsels or associate general counsels in charge of litigation at *seventy-nine* different corporations, most of them Fortune 500s. Every one of these meetings took place in the weeks and months that followed.

I later came to realize that this experience served as an ideal beta test for my system, allowing me to add the final tweaks and refinements, so that it could be packaged and taught to others.

Then I used my system on the publishing industry—another business that's notorious for being difficult to break into—in order to get my book published. I targeted eleven of the largest and best-known publishers; five granted the access I requested, and St. Martin's Press bought the book. They, too, were surprised at how easily I was able to get in their door.

Now this powerful, step-by-step system can help *you* gain access to the people you want to see so that you can fulfill your own goals, desires, and dreams.

—Michael A. Boylan

How This Book Can Get You In

The Magnitude of the Problem
You're Faced With

Back in the 60s, 70s, and even 80s, it used to be that if you had a good product or service, or good qualifications for that job opening you read about in the Sunday paper, you had a reasonable chance of getting in the door. You'd write a well-written letter or make a polite, focused phone call, and that would get you an appointment, at which you'd present your abilities, your credentials, your product, or your service.

And if that didn't work at first, then some gentle persistence and good old-fashioned hard work would usually open the door.

Furthermore, back in those days, if you had good credentials—

or a decent track record, or a customer success story, or a referral—that alone was often sufficient to get you in the door.

And while we're being nostalgic, let's recall something else: All of this took place in a more or less congenial and courteous environment.

Well, those days are *dead*. They're history. The old strategies for getting in simply don't work as well anymore, if at all.

Welcome to the age of the information superhighway, the Internet, teleconferencing, video conferencing, voice mail, digital pagers, fax machines, mobile phones, voice response systems, e-mail, and hand-held automated personal attendants.

Welcome to the age of downsizing, reorganizations, TQM and teams, corporate restructuring, cost cutting, and doing more with less.

Welcome to upheaval and unrest, reduced loyalties between employees and their employers, and unending change—right in your prospect's work environment and right in your face—morning to night, day after day.

Welcome to a world where it's *tougher than it has ever been* to get in your prospect's door.

This is the world in which you must function, compete, and succeed.

It's not a rosy scenario. But it's definitely the reality of the 90s—and beyond.

The rules of the game of getting in have changed drastically. In order to get in the door today, you've got to trash your old strategies, tactics, and methods, and learn to do things differently.

This book will show you how.

This Book Is Your Solution

The Power to Get In has been written for one single purpose: to help get you in the door of your desired prospects faster, more effectively, and with less expense, so that you can increase your income and achieve better overall results.

In this book I'll introduce you to the Circle of Leverage System, a step-by-step approach and execution philosophy that has proven highly successful, over and over, in business, politics, community affairs, and everyday life. It's a new way of thinking about gaining access. It is both extremely effective and 100 percent ethical. It's based on more than fifteen years of documented experience and success. And when properly executed, it can help anyone to get in the door of their desired prospects, regardless of their position or level of experience.

By "get in the door" I mean precisely this:

- Blast your way through all of the blockades set up to keep you out, at whatever level your prospect happens to be.

- Get access to the right person—the person who has the power to buy your product or service, hire you, approve your idea, or make some other decision in your favor.

- Be allowed to present your product, service, or idea to this person in the way *you* want to present it.

- Get your prospect's full attention and get them to make a decision on what you have to offer as quickly as possible.

In addition, this book will help you to:

- Create a far more influential power base and referral network, because you'll be getting in at much higher levels.

- Increase your income with less stress.

- Win more business deals, job interviews, and/or job offers, because you'll be getting in more often, with more confidence and control.

- Spend more time with "movers and shakers."

- If you're a salesperson or business executive, reduce your prospecting cycle—possibly your closing cycle as well—and in turn reduce your sales expenses.

- Have more fun in the process of getting in the door.

- Improve the quality of your life, because your income should go up and your stress level down.

14

The Circle of Leverage System can be effective and successful for you, even if you currently have no leverage whatsoever—no referral, no track record, no customer success stories, no existing personal or business relationship with your prospect, and no connection through a friend of the family.

If you use this system faithfully and correctly, this book will pay for itself *hundreds* of times over, either through increased commissions or income from your job, or from the new job that it will help you to obtain.

This Book Fits All Situations

When properly used, The Circle of Leverage System can work in virtually any situation, regardless of:

- The type of product or service you're selling—even if what you're selling is yourself

- The cost of your product or service

- The length of your sales cycle

- The title or level or responsibility you have in your current job (or in the job you hope to get)

- The title or level of responsibility your prospect has

- The complexities and nuances involved in selling your particular product or service, or yourself

- The educational credentials you do or don't have

- The number of other people who are competing for the business, job, or sale

- How long you've been in your current position (or how long you've been out of the work force)

The Circle of Leverage System is not some snake oil salesperson's approach to schmoozing your way in the door. It is a bold, straightforward, honest, 100 percent ethical approach— and the *only* approach that continues to work, time after time,

in today's difficult, closed-door, and often hostile business environment.

This book will dispel some of the BS you've previously been taught about what's proper and correct about getting in your prospect's door. It will empower you by giving you the right tools, the right information (much of which will likely be new to you), the right foundations, the right outlook, and the right stepping stones, so that you can navigate your way in your prospect's door, regardless of the situation you're in.

You Will Benefit Over and Over from This Book

I've written this book for all of the following people:

- Business owners, sales and marketing professionals, managers, and key executives in companies of *all* sizes, both private and publicly held

- People who have recently graduated (or will soon graduate) from college, graduate or professional school, or technical training programs

- Anyone looking for (or planning to look for) a new or better job

- Anyone who wants to return to the work force, or enter it for the first time

- Anyone who wants to achieve better results in their professional or personal life

If you fall into one or more of these categories, *The Power to Get In* can and will benefit you enormously.

What This Book Is Not

This book is *not* about how to sell or present a product, a service, an idea, or yourself. *It's about making sure you get the **chance** to present it.* This is *not* a Sales and Marketing 101 book.

This is *not* a book of generalized principles on how to succeed in business or life, or a volume of war stories detailing my personal triumphs and successes.

The Power to Get In will give you the background, tools, and training you need to craft your own unique, customized strategy for getting in your prospect's door. This book provides all the ingredients you need. It's a basic recipe for getting in; you will then alter and customize that recipe to suit your individual circumstances.

I can't and won't give you a guarantee that The Circle of Leverage System will work for you in every single situation with every single prospect. No approach is that good. Nothing in life works all the time. But I *can* guarantee that if you employ the Circle of Leverage System correctly, it *will* get you in *many more doors*—including some that were bolted shut and had "Absolutely Do Not Disturb" signs hung on them. It will also get you through doors that you were unwilling to even knock on before, because you felt your chances of getting in were slim to nonexistent.

Once you do get in, I can't guarantee that you'll win every sale or be offered every job you interview for. Obviously, I have no control over that. But if you can't even get in the door to the correct audience, your chances of closing that sale or getting that desired job are zero! *The Power to Get In* will therefore *dramatically increase your probability of success* by giving you a real chance to show your prospect what you have to offer.

Correct Leverage + Proper Execution = Success

I've developed and refined the Circle of Leverage System over the past fifteen years. It has provided me with access to many powerful and influential people, including the presidents and senior executives of many of America's largest corporations, among them General Motors, AT&T, ITT, Prudential, RJR Nabisco, American Express, Citicorp, Johnson & Johnson, PaineWebber, SmithKline Beecham, Time Warner, Pfizer, Amway Corporation, The Equitable, USX Corporation, PPG Industries, Mellon Bank, The Travelers, Chase Manhattan Bank, Chemical Bank, Tenneco Oil, Household Finance International, Shell Oil, BASF Corporation, Conoco Oil, and many, many others.

The Circle of Leverage System has also enabled me to build my own training and consulting company, The Boylan Group, Inc., through which I lead training seminars and coach people on how to get in their prospects' doors faster, more effectively, and with less expense, so that they increase their incomes and achieve better overall results.

The Circle of Leverage System has provided me with great success. It can provide you with great success as well, regardless of the profession you work in (or hope to work in).

As you will see, the Circle of Leverage System is so very exciting because it's real, honest, and ethical, and because it *works*, time after time after time.

What's Been Keeping You Out

One

Why You've Been Frozen Out

The Grim Reality

You've been frozen out, or are being frozen out right now. You can see it, feel it, almost taste it. And it's painful. At a minimum, it's a hassle—a total inconvenience.

You might find it comforting to know that most people who have something to sell, present, or offer feel the very same pain. But the specific reasons *why* you can't seem to get your foot in the door differ from person to person and from situation to situation. Let me give you a few examples.

If you're *a salesperson, a business owner, a manager, or a top executive for an industry leader*—a "major player" in your field—you may be getting frozen out because:

- Your household name, track record, powerful history, and customer success stories don't seem to mean as much to your prospects as they used to—at least, they're not delivering the automatic audience they used to.

- All of your direct competitors—the other firms your prospects are considering—are *also* major players in your field.

- Your prospects view your product or service as basically the same as what your competitors offer, no matter how unique its features or functions are and no matter how many clear, quantifiable benefits it offers.

- Your organization's credibility in the marketplace no longer seems any greater than anyone else's.

- You find yourself having to present your offer, over and over, level by level, to one person after another in the same organization, yet *few* of these people actually have the authority to say yes to your offer.

- You find yourself getting in the door at lower and lower levels than you used to, forcing you to present more "dog and pony shows" to non–decision makers.

If you're *a salesperson, a business owner, a manager, or a top executive at a lesser-known organization,* you may be getting frozen out because:

- Your product, service, or company is an unknown in your market, or at least unknown to your prospect.

- You (or your company) have no history, no track record, no referrals, or no existing relationships to use to get in.

- When your prospect issues a Request For Proposals, your company's name is not on it—which means you don't even have *permission* to submit a proposal or bid.

- You keep getting kicked down to a non–decision maker, where you then get blocked.

- You have no real leverage or power base to draw on.

- Your prospect's perception of your product or service is that it's a commodity—no different from what's offered by your competition—so all they're interested in is getting the best price.

- Even though you've gotten in a door, you've discovered that the all-important decision is made at a much higher level— and you can't seem to get to that level, for whatever reason.

- It seems to take longer than ever to close a sale, get a routine approval, or even get people to make *any* kind of decision. Sometimes it takes forever just to get a phone call returned, if it's returned at all.

- For whatever reason, it seems that your prospect isn't taking you seriously, perhaps is even treating you like you're a pest.

If you are *looking to make a job or career change,* or if you're *trying to enter or re-enter the job market,* you may be getting frozen out because:

- You have trouble standing out from the flood of applicants.

- Many of the people competing for the same jobs you are have more job experience or credentials than you do—sometimes much more.

- You have a hard time figuring out how to position yourself and your skills to potential employers.

- You often get irritated and angry at the general fakiness of some people in the business world.

- It's difficult for you to get psyched up to play the business game just to get a job.

- After finally getting through to someone in the personnel department, you find out that you are one of hundreds of people applying for the same job—and you never even get called in for an interview.

- You did what you thought you were supposed to do—cut out the ads that looked promising, sent a letter and your résumé to the proper addresses, and made follow-up calls. But almost nobody responded, and most didn't even have the decency to return your phone calls or acknowledge receipt of your materials.

And *no matter who you are*, you may also be getting frozen out because:

- Corporate takeovers, mergers, reorganizations, and downsizing are causing your prospects to be worried about their own jobs . . . their own security.

- The people you're trying to see seem to have less and less authority to make decisions.

- Your prospects seem to be more and more scared of making the wrong decision, which often means they make *no* decision.

- Your prospects have less time, are under more demands, and seem less tolerant than ever before.

- You can't get to the ultimate decision maker(s) because they're insulated from you by "the committee," or by an army of executive secretaries.

- Even though you were told who the decision maker supposedly is, often they're *not* the person who actually ends up making the decision. All too often they're just part of a committee, and that committee may itself not have the power to make a decision, but only a recommendation.

- On any given day, your prospects are probably *not* interested in granting access—an appointment, a conference call, a video conference, etc.—so they can learn more about how your offer might help them.

- The benefits of your offer, regardless of how wonderful they are, rarely provide enough of an incentive anymore to convince prospects to grant you access.

What Are the Forces Behind the Freeze-Out?

None of this has come about by accident. Three distinct trends have combined to cause more and more doors to slam shut.

Your prospects have become increasingly distrustful—and for good reason. If it's not already obvious to you how pervasive this lack of trust has become, ask yourself how much you trust telemarketers, insurance salespeople, lawyers, car dealers, or any stranger who is trying to gain access to you. Furthermore, your prospect has probably been stung more than once by people and organizations they weren't familiar with—or, at the very least, knows others who have been stung. They also believe you'll say just about *anything*, no matter how impossible or untrue, just to get in their door. Combine these things with the dramatic increase in sales scams across the country—including some by nationally known Fortune 1000 companies—and it's no surprise that more and more people have closed their doors. They've chosen to deal only with those organizations and individuals they already know very well—or that are brought to their attention through trusted referrals.

Competition has become much more fierce and often global—and it's getting steadily tougher. Whether you're looking to sell a product or service or simply get a job, you are battling enormous competition, often from around the country, sometimes from around the world. Because of this competitiveness, your prospect has much more power over you and far more options to choose from than ever before—which means they're able to be far more selective about the products, services, and people they grant access to.

Many people are seriously stressed out and often demoralized by rapid, continuous, pervasive change. Add in the pressures of cost cutting, steadily declining job security, and the ever-present bottom line, and it's no wonder that people have become edgy, uptight, less able to cope, and harder to deal with.

Put all of these things together and it's easy to understand why you—and so many others—have been (and continue to be) frozen out. Furthermore, the problem continues to get bigger and bigger.

Is There Any Good News?

Yes. *The Power to Get In* will give you the tools and strategies that will enable you to overcome *every one* of these killer situations. No matter how many of these problems are staring you in the face, this book will benefit you big time.

And there's more good news. Getting in the door is essentially a game—and, as with all games, there's a way to win. In the chapters to come I'll show you exactly how to play—and how to obtain the prize. In the process, you'll discover that the Circle of Leverage System makes the game much more fun and rewarding to play.

In Summary:

You've been frozen out because:

- Your prospects have become distrustful.

- Competition has become much fiercer and is getting fiercer still.

- People are seriously stressed out and demoralized by rapid, continuous, and pervasive change.

But there is hope. Getting in people's doors is a game, and this book will teach you how to win it.

Two

If You Can't Get In,
You Don't Have a Prayer

You Are a Persuader

E very one of us is in the persuasion business.

It doesn't matter what you do for a living (or what you hope to do). The fact is, certain parts of *every* job require you to persuade others to do certain things, to do them in certain ways, to work with you productively, and to listen to you and take you seriously.

All of this is every bit as true in our personal lives. We're almost *constantly* trying to persuade other people to do things—clean up their bedrooms, hurry up and get ready for school, pick up the dry cleaning, call us back as soon as possible, prepare our salad with the dressing on the side, and so on.

In fact, we've been persuading others to do what we want from the time we were born. And the interesting thing is that we were probably most successful at it when we were infants. Back then, we were master manipulators. A good pout, a little whine, or an all-out cry usually got us what we wanted: attention, food, someone to hold us. As we grew up, our life experiences shaped the ways we persuade people to listen to us and do what we want.

Getting In Is Everything

The Circle of Leverage System is a specific pattern of persuasion. It's partly about developing your own natural, inborn talent as a persuader (and, yes, we *all* have some of this talent). But it's much more about putting into play a series of specific steps and strategies that, in and of themselves, are incredibly persuasive—indeed, virtually unstoppable.

Why are these steps and strategies so important? Because *if you can't get in the door, you have no opportunity*. We're not talking about a slim chance. We're talking *none. Zero. Zip. Nada.*

If you can't get in to see the right person at the right time, it doesn't matter whether you're trying to sell yourself, your company's product or service, a great new idea, or even a cure for cancer. If the right people aren't listening, there's absolutely no point in talking. You're wasting your time.

The Circle of Leverage System is all about getting the right person (or people) to listen at the most opportune moment, so that you can deliver the presentation *you* wish to deliver, in the manner in which *you* want to deliver it.

It's got nothing to do with strong-arming or heavy-handed tactics. It's about causing them to *want* to pay attention to you and your request for access.

Everyone Can Benefit

At this point, maybe you're thinking, "Wait. I'm not a great talker or schmoozer. I'm not particularly good at coming up with the right words for any given situation."

Relax. The C.O.L. can work for every personality type and for people with every level of verbal skill. You don't have to be naturally extroverted or outgoing. In fact, I have specifically written this book for people of all levels of ability and experience. The C.O.L. will help you by starting from whatever point you're at right now, no matter what your personality traits are.

This brings us to one of the key principles behind the C.O.L.: *Getting in the door is* not *primarily a matter of personality or verbal skill. Nor is it primarily a matter of the particular product, service, or idea you have to offer.* Rather, *it's about understanding what truly motivates your prospect*—and using those needs, fears, and concerns as leverage to navigate your way in.

That's why the system works so well. Even if you're starting out with no leverage whatsoever, the system enables you to *create* and use leverage where previously you had none. *If you work the C.O.L. properly, it will work for you.*

In fact, throughout this book I'm going to assume you're starting out from a position of zero leverage. If you already have some leverage behind you—an inside contact, a strong referral, a track record, a good reputation—good for you. It *may* speed up the process of getting you in. *But you do not need to start out with any leverage whatsoever in order to use the C.O.L. successfully.* That's one of the best and most empowering things about it.

If you still have doubts about whether the C.O.L. can work for you, that's fine. You don't have to believe the principles it is built upon. The system will work if you apply and execute it properly— whether you think it will work or not!

Your ability to get in the door is as important as, if not more important than, the amount of knowledge you have about whatever it is you're offering. The next chapter looks at exactly why the traditional approach to getting in the door—the one we've all been taught is appropriate, and the one just about everyone has been using—has become so very ineffective.

In Summary:

- Everyone is in the persuasion business—and we've been in it all our lives.

- The Circle of Leverage System is a specific pattern of persuasion.

- The C.O.L. is based on what truly motivates your prospects: their needs, fears, and concerns. . . the things we've all been trained and conditioned to respond to since our birth.

- The C.O.L. can work for you regardless of your personality type or level of verbal skill.

- To use the C.O.L., you don't need to start out with any leverage whatsoever.

Three

Why the Bottom-Up Approach
Doesn't Work Anymore

Tried and True—or Tired and Useless?

Here is what I mean by the bottom-up approach:
    You get in touch with someone who represents an organization you want to connect with. Your goal is to sell something, get hired, obtain their assistance, or simply get your ideas heard. By letter, by phone, or in person you make your presentation about what you (or your product or service) can do for them. It's a good presentation, and in it you make very clear how what you have to offer can be of value and benefit to them.

    If you're lucky, and if your prospect responds well to your presentation, then you've made a sale, gotten the job, or obtained the assistance you're looking for. Right?

    Wrong! You already know—most likely from experience—what

usually happens next. You don't yet get what you're after. Instead, you get the chance to make your presentation again, to someone higher up in the chain of command.

Think about this for a moment. *If* you're very good, and *if* the person you made your presentation to was paying enough attention to realize that you have something valuable to offer, then *your reward is the chance to do it all over again with somebody else.*

And you already know what often happens after that. If this "somebody else" is impressed by your second presentation—and if they have the time, the willingness, the interest, the authority, and the gumption to pursue your proposal within the organization—do you *then* get the job, the sale, or the assistance?

Most likely not yet. It's probable that you'll now be offered the opportunity to make presentation number three. And while there's a chance that you'll be speaking to some of the same people you've dealt with already, it's more likely that you'll be going before one or more strangers. And for these people you'll have to start from scratch with your presentation yet again.

Sounds familiar, doesn't it?

May I remind you that what I've just described is *the best-case scenario* for anyone who is following the bottom-up approach? This is what might happen *if you and your prospect do everything right*— and if you're lucky, to boot. And notice that you still haven't gotten the sale, the job, or the assistance you're after.

But let's say that you've made presentation #3, and it's gone quite well. You've done a good job of positioning yourself (and/or the product or service you're offering), and you've clearly demonstrated that what you're offering your prospect addresses their needs, goals, and objectives very well. You've created a groundswell of support, and it's looking like your prospect will make a decision in your favor.

But all too often, here's what happens next:

Along comes your competition—either another company in the same industry, or someone else who wants the same job or assistance you do. Only they're coming in with a difference. They've got a connection, a referral, or some other "in." Maybe they play golf with the head of the company. Or maybe they've done business with (or worked for) the organization before. Or maybe they're the boss's nephew. Whatever the connection, they breeze in at a level way above where you began—and most likely above where you are now—and quickly sew up the deal, the job, or the assistance.

And where does this leave you? Dead in the water.

This doesn't happen every time, of course. But it does happen often enough that I'll bet you predicted it as you were reading.

The strange thing is, if you consider exactly what the bottom-up approach is, it's obvious why it is so ineffective. The bottom-up approach involves *approaching the person with the least amount of power, authority, and decision-making ability*—and then slowly working your way up to the person (or people) with the greatest amount of power, authority, and decision-making ability.

Most of us have been taught to prospect one person at a time, make our best effort, then follow up for a response. If the answer is "no, thank you," we often try to find a sympathetic ear elsewhere within the same company, or else reprospect at a later date.

In other words, the bottom-up approach is just about the slowest, most indirect, and most roundabout approach you can take. No wonder it's so ineffective. Nevertheless, it's what most of us have been taught as the proper way to do things.

The bottom-up approach doesn't fail in 100 percent of all circumstances, but in recent years its success rate has dropped closer and closer to zero. If your competition doesn't have the right connections, or if they can't offer all the benefits you can, you *might* still get what you're after. But if your competition *does* get in at a much higher level, and if their offer is as good as what you're presenting, and if their presentation is as strong as yours, there's a better than 50 percent chance that they'll end up with the job, the sale, or the assistance you worked so hard to obtain. And you'll have wasted a great deal of time, money, effort, and energy—yours *and* your prospect's. And that leaves a bad taste in everyone's mouth.

Why Bang Your Head Against a Closed Door?

The great majority of people who use the bottom-up approach don't even get that first meeting, the initial interview, or that crucial phone call. They don't get blocked at step two, three, or four, because they don't make it past step one.

Let's recap why the bottom-up approach has always created problems:

- It forces you to pass through level after level, making presentation after presentation, just to *reach* the person or group that actually makes a decision on what you have to offer.

- You can be turned away at *any* one of these levels, for *innumerable* reasons, many of which have nothing to do with you or with what you're offering.

- *Every single one of your competitors* with an inside connection or referral gets in more easily or gets more attention, and therefore has an enormous advantage over you—*every step of the way.*

- Every hour of effort you expend in presenting and re-presenting your offer to the wrong audience is an hour wasted.

- You leave too much—*way* too much—to chance every step of the way.

- You're the person with the *least* amount of control over the process—*and the outcome.*

Actually, to some degree everything I've described so far has been true for a long time. The bottom-up approach has always been a statistical game, the idea being that if you try it enough times, with enough prospects, eventually you'll obtain what you're after. And years ago, it worked often enough to make the bottom-up approach somewhat effective.

But not anymore. Things have changed. Greater competition, advanced technology, more sophisticated sales techniques, and much greater distrust among your prospects have made things much tougher than ever.

Here are some reasons why the bottom-up approach is far less effective in the 90s than it has ever been before, and why it will continue to grow less and less effective in the 2000s—reasons that are clearly visible everywhere:

- **Prospects today face massive amounts of change—and, as a result, must handle more stress, anxiety, and uncertainty than ever before.** Some of this change is technological or cultural; some is the result of corporate reengineering, restructuring, and downsizing.

- **Because of the increased litigiousness of our society, people in most businesses are more cautious, frustrated, and sometimes numb.** In their eyes it doesn't matter who you are; all that matters is that you're trying to gain access to them, that you want something from them. That scares or irritates them, so you're simply viewed as someone to deal with cautiously and at a distance. Or you may be ignored entirely, simply because it may seem safest to do nothing.

- **Most businesspeople are required to be away from their offices far more than ever before.** Many do some work at home; many routinely make and take calls from their cars, while on the move. These days, simply locating people, let alone pinning them down in one spot for an appointment, has become an exercise in frustration. Try to put three or four people together in one room at once, and the scheduling problems grow exponentially.

- **Businesses are making far wider use of outside consultants, who often insert themselves in the midst of the decision-making process.** As a result, you must not only convince someone *within* the organization that you're worth listening to, but you must also convince the outside consultant. This doubles the effort you must expend while cutting your chances for success in half.

- **Today there are fewer true leaders who want or welcome responsibility and who are willing to take a stand or express an opinion.** Many people in large and midsize organizations want less and less ownership and accountability; instead, all they really want is to keep their jobs and get by for another day. The result once again is that you must go higher and higher to find someone with the courage to take a position. In short, there exists *a pervasive and chronic lack of lead-*

ership. Because of the turbulent and shark-infested waters most managers must operate in today, people are more concerned than ever before with covering their butts. They fear making the wrong decision, so often they make no decision. As a result, more and more decisions are driven higher and higher within organizations, or are "committeed" to death. Many more decisions are now being made by task forces or committees rather than one individual. But committees are often as scared about making a decision as one or two people. So they often recommend two or three "final candidates," then kick the decision to a higher level.

- **Of necessity, people and their organizations have become more competitive than ever before.** Many are getting to be ruthless, willing to do whatever it takes to get their way.

- **Most people simply have less time to give to you, or to almost anyone.**

It's become a kind of war zone out there. And the old bottom-up approach has simply become inadequate. If you're serious about getting in the door, you're going to need a new way of thinking and a very different approach, an approach that takes *all* of these realities into account, an approach that genuinely *works.*

That approach is the Circle of Leverage System.

In Summary:

- The bottom-up approach means contacting the person with the least amount of power, authority, and decision-making ability, then slowly working your way up.

- With the bottom-up approach, you have to do your dog and pony show over and over, time after time—*if* you're lucky enough not to be sent away.

- Even if you do begin to work your way up, at any time your competition can come in with a referral or contact and blow you out of the water. This leaves you with very little control over your destiny.

- The bottom-up approach is slow, indirect, and usually ineffective—which is why it is becoming obsolete.

- Today a completely new and different approach is needed. The C.O.L. is that approach.

Four

The High-Tech Freeze-Out

Ten years ago very few businesses had voice-mail systems, fax machines, or elaborate computer networks. Only a handful of people routinely used mobile phones, digital pagers, or computer notebooks. And there was no such thing as the Internet, the World Wide Web, caller ID, or electronic mail.

A scant decade later it is difficult to imagine a successful business that doesn't rely on dozens of forms of electronic wizardry simply to complete its normal day-to-day tasks. It's not just that we expect to have quick access to fax machines, personal computers, voice mail, E-mail, cellular phones, on-line services, the Internet, and the World Wide Web wherever we turn. Today, most of us literally couldn't run our businesses without them.

And for all that we've totally wired, microchipped, E-mailed, Internetted, and cellularized ourselves, everyone knows that the future will be even more technology-dependent than it is now.

Question: Have all of these forms of "access" made it easier for you to meet and talk with the people you most want to reach—or have they made it harder than ever?

Another brain-twister for you: Will the ever-faster growth of "communications" technology soon make in-person and voice-to-voice contact next to impossible?

By now you've accepted the fact that, day in and day out, you must somehow compete and survive in a war zone. But there's something else that you must understand as well: *Each of your potential prospects must also compete and survive in that same war zone.*

And what are the first things most people do when they feel under attack? Build walls and hide behind them.

This is *exactly* what most of your prospects have done. Today, most businesses have erected virtual fortresses around themselves through the use of new technologies, from voice mail to on-line services to caller ID. While one purpose of these systems is to help people connect with one another more easily and quickly, another purpose is to keep out the people they don't know, or don't want to know.

Just what is it that they are trying so hard to guard and protect? Simple: *their time*—the most valuable thing any of us has.

Think of all the times you've tried to make contact with someone who simply hid from you or refused to respond. It's terribly frustrating, because all the other person has to do is nothing. By simply ignoring you, they can freeze you out as if you don't even exist—even though there might be incredibly good reasons why they *should* talk with you. Worse, you'll never find out what their reason is for ignoring you.

This has always been true to some degree. But as technology has advanced, the situation has gotten *much* worse. For example, in the past, people hid behind their secretaries. If someone wanted you to go away, they'd have their secretary tell you that they were in conference, on another line, or simply unavailable, and the secretary would take a message. This was difficult and frustrating, but at least you were talking with a human being—someone who could be questioned, reasoned with, and sometimes coaxed into helping you. And you at least knew that your messages were getting through, even if they were being ignored. Plus there was always the chance that the secretary would be away from their desk and that their boss—your prospect—would pick up the phone.

Today, however, even those small comforts are disappearing. Nowadays, if someone doesn't want to talk with you, you're usually stuck with leaving a recorded message. You can't ask a voice mail message a question, or reason with it, or coax it into helping you. In fact, you can't be sure your message has gotten through in the first place. You're trying to make contact in a vacuum.

True, plenty of people today still have secretaries and assistants. But most people have voice mail as well. So do their secretaries. Which means that if they want to hide from you, they have no less than three buffers between them and you.

Of course, voice mail is just the beginning. Virtually every month some new technology appears that makes it even easier to freeze you out. In mid-1995, caller ID was introduced in my city. Now, for a few dollars a month, I can tell who's calling me without picking up my phone. If I want to avoid you, all I need to do is glance at an LED display, then return to what I was doing—while you get stuck in a voice mail maze.

Everywhere you go, your prospects are using the tools of technology to erect a thicker and thicker buffer between themselves and you, making it ever tougher for you to gain access. *The technological innovations that were supposed to make our lives easier and create more opportunities for making connections are also being used as sophisticated methods of defense and avoidance.*

Here's another example: fax machines. They've enabled us to save enormous amounts of time, and they allow us to transfer data of all types quickly and efficiently. But they are also used as a way of avoiding human contact. Think how many in-person meetings have been replaced with flurries of faxes and phone calls—or, at best, conference calls or video conferences.

The result of all this technology is that flesh-and-blood, person-to-person meetings are becoming rarer and rarer. Yet, as *any* salesperson or lobbyist can tell you, if you can't get a face-to-face meeting with someone, you're usually dead in the water, because you can't generate that all-important rapport.

What can the traditional bottom-up approach do to help you deal with these difficult and frustrating situations? Absolutely nothing.

But by using the Circle of Leverage System, you *can* do something about the ever-thickening technological walls. First, you can use the system to cut right through most or all of the technological buffers, so that you get quick, direct, in-person access to the person or people you've targeted. Second, you can make some of the technological buffers your prospects have erected work to *your* benefit instead of theirs.

Later chapters of this book will give you the specific tools you need to deal effectively with people's electronic fortresses.

In Summary:

- We've created an E-mailed, Internetted, microchipped, cellularized world—a world that is going to be even more technology-dependent in the future.

- Your prospects now use these new, sophisticated forms of increased communication as additional barriers between you and them.

- These high-tech methods of defense and avoidance have rendered the traditional approach virtually useless.

- The Circle of Leverage System can help you cut quickly and cleanly through these technological barriers—and even use them to your advantage.

THE CIRCLE OF LEVERAGE SYSTEM: WHAT IT IS, WHAT'S BEHIND IT, AND HOW IT WORKS

Five

Why the Top-Down Approach Works

The Voice of Power

I t's true that money talks. *But power shouts.*

Imagine you're a middle manager in a Fortune 1000 corporation. One morning you find four memos on your desk—one from accounting, one from your counterpart in another division, one from your secretary, and one from your company's chief operating officer. Each one asks you to immediately carry out a different task. Which task are you going to complete first?

Or suppose you're a private in the Army. You receive simultaneous orders from three different people: a corporal, a lieutenant, and a general. Whose order are you going to follow first?

The higher up someone is in an organization, the more other people in that organization will usually listen to them or care about what they think. Therefore, if you can align yourself with someone influential and come in from the top down, you can actually borrow some of that person's power and authority to leverage open people's doors.

The top-down approach enables you to circumvent most of the people, technologies, and systems that have been put in place to keep you out. It immediately separates you from most or all of your competitors. And it greatly increases your chances of getting in by ensuring that you are routed quickly to the right people.

Coming in from the top down dramatically increases the possibility that people will want to pay attention to you. And the higher the level at which you do get in, the more likely you are to achieve your objectives.

Of course, using the top-down approach doesn't necessarily mean starting out by approaching the president or CFO. Rather, it means starting out *one to three levels above your prospect*, so that when you arrive for your first appointment, you are meeting with the correct decision maker(s).

The Traditional Top-Down Approach and the Circle of Leverage

Think back to some of the times when you were passed over or pushed aside in favor of someone else who had inside connections or influence—the boss's nephew, the general manager's old college roommate, or the division head's neighbor or golfing buddy or significant other. You were probably disappointed, angry, and jealous because your competition had it so easy. And you probably thought of yourself as a victim of favoritism, nepotism, string pulling, or the old-boy network.

These are all examples of the same thing: gaining access from the top down.

"And that's exactly my problem," you say. "I *can't* come in from the top down because I don't have an inside track, or an old-boy contact, or some other connection."

True, you may not have an inside contact. But you *can* still come in from the top down in a different way—by using the C.O.L. to apply subtle yet effective emotional pressure on your prospects.

The C.O.L. enables you to borrow and use leverage *that is already in place* within your prospect's organization—even though you may have zero leverage of your own.

The leverage that already exists in your prospect's organization—leverage that *you* can borrow from—includes:

- The authority of superiors

- The threat of competition, from both inside and outside of your prospect's organization

- Insecurity and curiosity about who else you are involved with, and who else is paying attention to you

- Fear of losing power, authority, or influence

- Fear of becoming unimportant, of being left out of the process

- Fear of losing credibility

- Fear of looking stupid or out of touch

- Fear of losing others' respect and trust

- Fear of losing a raise or promotion

- Fear of job loss

Think about those times in the past when you got the access you wanted through the assistance of an insider with whom you had some prior connection or relationship. In each case, that person made a conscious decision to help you, a decision that was based primarily on a feeling. That feeling might have been friendship, responsibility, loyalty, goodwill, duty, or even guilt. Whatever it was, *they made an emotional decision to act on your behalf.*

The C.O.L. also causes your prospects to make emotional decisions to act on your behalf. (Later on, they may also discover more rational reasons to do so as well.) However, in place of loyalty, responsibility, etc., your prospects act out of insecurity, anxiety, or fear of loss. They act or react to avoid potential painful consequences.

47

These two top-down approaches have something else in common: *In each case, your prospect ultimately **wants** to grant you access, because they come to see that doing so is in their own best interest—a way to avoid something they don't want.*

Coercion vs. Desire

A paradox faces everyone who wants to get in someone else's door. On the one hand, your prospects want to keep you out (at least at first) because you're a stranger, an unknown quantity, and therefore almost certainly unnecessary to them. On the other hand, the only way for them to really find out if you can benefit them is for them to let you in—which is the one thing they least want to do.

A second paradox rests on the first. The very reason you want access in the first place is to show your prospects how much what you have to offer can help them. If only you could get their attention for a few minutes, they'd very likely be interested in what you're offering. But you can't get their attention because they just plain don't want to listen.

You're caught in both of these frustrating double binds. And at the heart of both of these paradoxes is human desire—*wanting*.

The reason you're reading this book is that *many of your desired prospects don't want to see or talk with you.* If they did, you could pick up the phone and schedule all the appointments you wanted.

You can deal with this reality in one of two ways. You can do what most people do, which is to try to convince your prospect to meet with you, *even though they don't want to.* Or you can *get your prospect to **want** to let you in.*

The C.O.L. uses forthright and honest communication—and power drawn from existing relationships—to actually change how your prospects *feel* about granting you access. The C.O.L. works not by bullying your way inside over your prospect's objections—which usually doesn't work, anyway (and when it does, it leaves a bad taste in your prospect's mouth)—but by making them *want* to open their door to you.

It does this by demonstrating to your prospects—clearly, quickly, dramatically, and undeniably—that they may have *far* more to lose by freezing you out than by letting you inside. It pushes the right emotional buttons at the right time—not in a rude or abusive way, but straightforwardly, honestly, and directly, so that your prospects' desires automatically come into alignment with your own.

Stimulus and Automatic Response

The Circle of Leverage employs the very same types of stimuli we have been raised on—and have been trained to respond to—since we were very small kids.

It's funny. Everyone agrees that our adult behavior and responses are largely shaped by our early childhood. Yet we've forgotten about these powerful and automatic learned responses when it comes to getting in people's doors. We completely ignore these virtually universal reactions. Instead, we concentrate on presenting the net benefits of what we have to offer as the key reasons and the justification for why our prospects should allow us in the door.

I'm sure many of you have already experienced something like this: You've got a product to offer—a computer system, let's say—that is the best in the business. You're excited about it, because it delivers great value to the customer. It's faster, more efficient, easier to use, and longer lasting than anything the competition has to offer. Not only that, it's 35 percent cheaper than any of your competitors' products. Plus, maybe it's backed by the best warranty or one of the most prestigious names in the industry.

You're savvy enough to know that, obviously, not every prospect who hears about these benefits will buy from you. But these clear-cut, quantifiable, *obvious* benefits should at least make many of your prospects say, "Okay, come on in and make your half-hour presentation." So you're absolutely shocked and amazed that when you present these *blatant* benefits to most of your prospects in a phone call or letter, *they seem to make no impression whatsoever.* In fact, your prospects seem to have no interest at all in helping their organizations succeed. You're feeling a tad frustrated, like maybe your prospect doesn't have the light on . . . or perhaps is just plain stupid. You're thinking, "Who in their right mind wouldn't want to hear about these fantastic and genuine benefits?"

The problem here, of course, is that we all assume that our prospects will "get it"—that they'll see the light. And the simple fact is that often they won't, because they're waiting for something else that they don't even realize they're waiting for. They're waiting for a certain type of stimulus to be introduced to them . . . the very same one they're used to responding to since birth. And that is the presentation of an *immediate potential consequence*.

Now let's step back for a second and look at this failure to "get it" in another light. *Forget* the many benefits of your offer for a minute. Instead, let's focus on your prospect.

My question is this: Is there any *immediate* potential consequence—positive or negative—for your prospect if they choose not to respond to you, listen to you, or even care about you?

The answer is no. There is none.

What is most important to many (perhaps most) of your prospects on any given day is *not* the benefits of your offer. What is most important to them on any given day are *the relationships they have with their coworkers, superiors, subordinates, and direct competitors*. Therefore, the more that you involve these other people in your strategy for getting in the door, the more likely your prospects are to pay attention to you, because these relationships they've built are paramount to them.

Furthermore, if you include in your strategy the same types of stimuli that we are all trained and conditioned to respond to since birth, you *dramatically* increase the potential of their automatically wanting to pay attention. As a result, you also dramatically increase your potential for getting in your prospects' doors.

It's really quite simple. Here's an example of what I'm talking about. When I was six or seven, my father would say to me, "Michael, time for dinner. Please turn off the TV and come upstairs." Naturally, I wouldn't respond because there was no potential consequence presented. "Michael, dinnertime. Please turn off the TV right now and come up." Again, no response, for the same reason. "Michael, if you don't turn off the TV immediately and come upstairs, you'll have to go to bed *right now*—without any dinner—and you won't be able to play with your friends until tomorrow." There it was: the consequence. It's what I was waiting for. Now I could weigh my choices and quickly respond to the choice that presented me with the least amount of pain. Naturally, I responded immediately by turning off the TV and going upstairs for dinner. Why? Because I knew there would be *an immediate, potentially painful consequence* if I didn't respond in the way my father wanted.

Since childhood, we've all been used to responding to the exact same type of stimuli. And, as adults, they're still the primary messages we react to, and the main forces that motivate us to act or react.

Don't believe me? Then ask yourself this: How many things do you (or others you know) put off until the very last minute? Isn't it true that you let them remain unattended to *up until that point when if you continue to ignore them, the consequences will be dire?* The *benefits* of acting aren't enough to motivate you. Only when the potential for painful consequences enters the scenario do you—like just about all of us—finally act or react.

Providing your prospects with these potential consequences must therefore become part of your strategy for getting in their doors. Subconsciously, they're all *waiting* for that stimulus—that message, that signal, that announced consequence—and when they are presented with it, they respond in an automatic, learned fashion, which they view as a normal response.

In the chapters to follow, you'll see exactly how this works.

In Summary:

- Coming in from the top down dramatically increases the possibility that people will want to pay attention to you.

- The higher up someone is in an organization, the more others in that organization care what they do, say, and think.

- If you can align yourself with an influential person in any organization, you can borrow some of their power to use as leverage.

- This leverage causes your prospect to *want* to grant you access, because they see that they have far more to lose by freezing you out than by letting you in.

- Most of your prospects are not as concerned with the benefits of your offer as they are with the relationships they have with their coworkers, superiors, subordinates, and direct competitors. Therefore, the more that you involve these other people in your strategy for getting in the door, the more likely your prospects are to pay attention to you.

- The Circle of Leverage employs the very same types of stimuli we have been raised on, and have been trained to respond to, since we were very small kids: *immediate, potentially painful consequences for not acting*. As adults, these remain the primary messages we react to, and the main forces that motivate us.

- Providing your prospects with these stimuli must therefore become part of your strategy for getting in their doors.

Six

The Essence of Leverage

Risk and Fear:
The Building Blocks of Leverage

Getting in the door of your desired prospects is really nothing more than a complex mental and emotional game—a high-level contest of power, timing, perceptions, and the consequences of those perceptions and actions. At the heart of this game are your prospect's fears, curious insecurities, competitive issues, and desires—what I call their four Key Engagers. The Circle of Leverage System is a direct, straightforward, carefully planned approach and execution strategy that engages these four elements and uses them to your benefit.

However, the C.O.L. is *not a* bullying approach or strong-arm tactic. It is a series of steps that, when properly executed, allow you to gain access to the person or people you've targeted.

The C.O.L. works by *creating leverage* where previously you had little or none. This leverage is, in essence, borrowed from *existing* power relationships that your prospect is caught up in. These relationships are paramount to your prospect. In fact, they're much more important to your prospect on any given day than the net benefits of your offer . . . tons more. They involve a person or people whom your prospect respects and responds to. The system then enables you to *surround your targeted prospect with the correct kind and amount of leverage.*

This circle of leverage you have created around your prospect triggers one or more of their four Key Engagers: their fears, their curious insecurities, their competitiveness, and their desire to be a serious player. Ultimately, it dramatically increases the probability that your targeted prospect will allow you access. Why? *Because you show your prospect that they could incur more risk by freezing you out than by letting you in.*

The C.O.L. is based on a high level of common sense. As a result, it is easy to remember and easy to execute. It consists of *ten Preparation Steps* and *five Execution Steps*, each of which will be presented in detail in the chapters to come. The system combines careful and thorough research about your prospect with your own judgment and experience to help you identify:

- Your prospect's pressure points

- Your prospect's natural fears and insecurities

- Your prospect's competitiveness issues

- Your prospect's desires to be a serious player

Once you have this information, you can use the steps and information in this book to build a targeted game plan for getting in the door of that prospect.

The C.O.L. is a powerful tool that is adaptable to a wide variety of people, situations, and organizations. But just because the system is flexible doesn't mean you can afford to be sloppy in using it. The system *must be used correctly.* If you don't follow all of the Preparation Steps, or don't correctly execute all of the Execution Steps, the system won't work as effectively—and your chances for success will decrease.

Please remember that the system is designed to be effective when you're starting out with no leverage at all: no relationship, no referral, no connection whatsoever to your prospect, no reputation, and no track record—nothing at all that would impress your prospect. I'll assume this is the situation you're in. If you already have a little bit of leverage, wonderful. The system will work all the better for you.

Rethinking Your Strategy

Imagine you're a general, and you and your military advisers are designing an attack on a fortified position. One of your officers makes this suggestion: "Let's attack the target with one soldier." You look at him as if he's crazy. "All right, then we'll attack it with one plane." Now you *know* he's crazy, and tell him so. "Okay, then, we'll fire one missile at it."

You can see immediately how useless—and suicidal—sending in just one of anything is going to be. *Yet that is exactly how most people approach the process of getting in the door.* They pick a single spot and go after it single-handedly. Then they wonder why they don't get results! The flip side is that your offer will more than likely benefit many people in your prospect's organization. Yet, because of our training, we still go at only one person at a time.

The fact is, your prospects are hidden behind fortified positions, just as if they are desirable military targets. They have secretaries, assistants, and other subordinates who are paid to keep you out. Plus, they have voice mail, fax machines, and other tools of modern technology to act as buffers. And often they've already decided that they don't *need* to see you or talk with you. They believe they've already got what you're offering, that they can get it elsewhere better or cheaper, or that they don't need it at all. And all the while, they're defending their position with multiple forces.

Given this situation, how much sense does it make for you to pick a single door and knock on it over and over?

With the C.O.L., you *never* target just one person at a time, because it's suicide. Instead, you target one *plus* two or three. You *identify a minimum of two or three people—called Leverage Points—who have some influence on your prospect.* This prospect is the person or group you really want access to, the one that actually has the power to say yes to your offer. *You then use these Leverage Points to surround your prospect with the proper amount and type of leverage, which helps motivate them to grant access.*

You will use the ten Preparation Steps to:

- Identify who each of these people is in your targeted organization

- Study the employer-employee relationships that already exist among these people

- Borrow some of the power *that already exists* in those relationships to create your leverage for getting in the door

- Most effectively position, package, and present your offer so that it is most attractive to your prospect (and to their Leverage Points)

You will then use the five Execution Steps to:

- Develop a customized attack strategy for those people and that organization

- Carry out that strategy

- As necessary, develop and implement additional maneuvers that make use of "side roads"; these maneuvers keep your leverage on your prospect strong, consistent, and "fresh"— until you are granted the access you need.

The Principles Behind the Circle of Leverage System

To use the C.O.L. effectively, you need to understand the principles it is based on. There are nine in all, each one intimately related to the stresses and forces your prospects must deal with every day.

1. **Hierarchies will always exist.** No matter how flat, horizontal, or trendy an organization supposedly is, there is always some basic hierarchical structure in place. The reason for this is simple: Without a hierarchy of some type—whether formal or informal, official or unofficial—nothing gets done. Some organizations disguise their actual hierarchies or make them harder to figure out, but the hierarchies are still there! Someone at each level will *always* be ultimately charged with responsibility—because work has to get done and decisions have to be made.

2. **Your prospects are unwilling—and often afraid—to respond.** Your prospects must cope with massive and constant change. This takes time, energy, flexibility, and courage. And while they're busy coping, they've still got their full-time jobs to attend to. As a result, many of your prospects are having serious trouble just keeping their heads above water. Their primary focus may be on just doing enough to get by. One of the fallback positions in such a high-stress situation is to do nothing or to become aloof and unresponsive.

3. **Your prospects are in information overload.** They are already so battered with information, demands, organizational politics, and all kinds of clutter that they have become (or are fast becoming) numb. Often their minds are so buzzed out with data and details that they are simply unable to respond to an outsider's request—unless they feel that *not* responding could result in a more painful consequence than responding. In other words, what makes them *want* to respond is the sense that they could incur greater risk by doing nothing than by letting you in their door.

4. **Your prospects suffer from a serious lack of leadership.** Many of your prospects are scared to think or act on their own beliefs and opinions. Many rely on committee decisions, where two or more people have to sign off, thus taking the responsibility off any one person's shoulders. In extreme cases, some of your prospects may have become robots. None of this is new—but in the 90s it has gotten much worse than before.

5. **Your prospects suffer from a lack of recognition.** Many of the people you're approaching feel unrecognized or unrewarded in their current positions. As a result, they may be angry, short-tempered, irritable, impatient, or even vindictive.

6. **Often your prospects just plain don't care.** It's no secret that for most managers, job security has shrunk to almost zero. Many organizations don't care as much about their employees as they used to (even though the corporate talk invariably says otherwise). It should therefore come as no surprise that many employees aren't terribly loyal to their employers—and they certainly aren't going to bend over backward for them. For many of your prospects, then, unless you and your offer will have a direct effect on *them*, personally or professionally, they don't give a hoot. From their point of view, you're a pest.

7. **Your prospects often have their own agendas, which may differ from their organizations' by as much as 180 degrees.** Don't let company mission statements fool you. Remember, a prospect is not the same as the organization they work for; each one is a person or a small group within that organization. And if they are primarily concerned with an agenda of their own, they may try to freeze you out for undisclosed reasons of their own. However, by using the C.O.L. properly, you can completely *envelop your prospects in their organizations' agendas*—which causes them to *want* to pay attention to you. Don't forget, your prospects are supposed to be operating in the best interests of their employers; the C.O.L. helps to bring them back to that reality.

8. **Many of your prospects are arrogant and out of touch.** You will come across prospects who say routinely, "I don't need to be involved in that meeting, thank you" or "My people will handle it and report back to me if there is anything I need to know." While it is true that good leaders are often excellent orchestrators and delegators, this kind of attitude can also come from a general unwarranted cockiness, laziness, or arrogance. This attitude, unfortunately, has become common at all levels, and is growing.

9. **The benefits of your offer, no matter how significant or obvious they may be, are not enough of an incentive for your prospects to grant you access.** Regardless of how wonderful your product, service, concepts, or abilities are—and regardless of how much good they can do for your prospects' organizations—it is foolish to believe that they are strong enough to make your prospects grant you access, or even pay attention to you. Your prospects may have any number of logical or illogical reasons why they don't want to see you—they're afraid of making a change, they doubt that what you're offering is any better than the competition, they're too busy dealing with emergencies or crises, or they're apprehensive about dealing with strangers. The specific reason isn't important; what's important is that, at this point, they're not interested in learning more about you or your offer, and they're certainly not about to say, "You're just what we need! Get in here!" *You must therefore structure and position your offer so that it presses their mental and emotional hot buttons—because nothing else is going to work.*

Your Sources of Real Leverage

In using the C.O.L., you will begin by analyzing the existing hierarchy in your prospect's organization—both the official one *and* the one that actually operates. (Sometimes they are different.)

Next, you will use the four Key Engagers described below to motivate your prospect. You'll do this *with your prospect and (usually) two or three other people* who have some direct or indirect influence over your prospect. These people will become your Leverage Points for getting your prospect to open the door to you.

Then you'll use the five Execution Steps described in Part IV to activate the Key Engagers of your prospect—*and*, simultaneously, of each of the Leverage Points you've identified. This enables you to flush out your ultimate prospect *in a top-down pattern*, with each Leverage Point adding leverage and momentum to your request for access. As the leverage and momentum build, a "funneling" effect is created, in which more and more pressure is brought to bear on this prospect, motivating them to want to grant the access you need.

Your Prospect's Four Key Engagers

Most of your prospects respect the power, authority, titles, job descriptions, and responsibilities that are already in place within their organizations. Often they respect a superior's title and position of authority far more than they respect the actual person. Typically, this is because they feel, deep down, that they could do their superior's job much better than their superior, if only they were given the chance.

Furthermore, it's likely that each of your prospects has already plotted out their own path for career advancement. But in order to advance—to get more money, more power, more responsibility, more recognition, more freedom, more of whatever it is that they value— they need *more visibility, more exposure*—usually both to people in the company and to customers or other outsiders. They need something that makes them stand out—whether it's the successful completion of a project, a cost-saving measure they instituted, a new idea that their bosses appreciate, a special initiative that is beneficial to the organization, or anything else both positive and significant.

In part, the C.O.L. draws its power from your prospects' need for this exposure. It works by engaging one or more of their four Key Engagers—emotional and mental hot buttons that you can use to cause them to act, react, and *want* to grant you the access you desire. These Key Engagers are your prospects':

1. Fear of loss

2. Curious insecurities

3. Competitiveness

4. Strong desire to be a "serious player"

Let's take a closer look at each of these Key Engagers.

1. **Fear of Loss.** When we were children, most of us occasionally teased, tormented, or bullied our siblings and playmates. We often kept going, no matter how much we were asked to stop, just to see how far we could get. We were flexing our muscles, exercising our power, trying to see how far our new domains could reach and how much influence we could exert over others.

It all worked great—until someone appealed to some higher authority (usually Mom or Dad), and that authority made us shape up. And we did shape up, most of the time, at least for the moment. Why? Because we feared punishment, which can be painful and embarrassing, and because we *needed* Mom and Dad for food, for clothes, for shelter, for protection, and most of all for love.

Now, notice: Most of us *didn't* shape up until somebody who had more authority engaged our fear of pain, or of some unwanted consequence. It took that authority *and* some sort of painful consequences (or, at least, the threat of those consequences) for us to stop what we were doing and pay attention.

We learned both this muscle-flexing behavior and this responsiveness to potential punishment extremely well at a *very* early age. And, for better or worse, as we got older, many of us continued with it—in school, with our own children, and, most of all, in the workplace. And on a day-to-day basis, many of us continue with pretty much the same behavior we learned as kids. In fact, it's become second nature for almost all of us—including your prospects.

When your prospects are freezing you out, they are often doing nothing more than flexing their muscles, exercising their power and influence over you for a variety of reasons. So how can you turn the tables and cause them to want to let you in their door? By involving yourself with people who have influence on them, thus *introducing the possibility of painful and pleasurable consequences*, like Mom and Dad did with you.

This is hardly childish behavior, however! Indeed, it is the very core of how and why we respond to many—perhaps most—of the things we encounter in our adult lives. It's what we all learned and accept as normal behavior to this very day.

One of the ways the C.O.L. works is by identifying and engaging the power of those people in an organization who can influence your prospect. In most cases, they must (1) hold a position senior or equal to your prospect, and/or (2) have a genuine influence on or over your prospect. When these people engage their power, they invoke in your prospect a fear of potential loss—loss of their superior's respect or approval, loss of a promotion, loss of their job, or loss of something they can't quite put their finger on. And in response to this fear, they will often make the decision—of their own free will—to grant you the access you need. At the same time, they *don't* feel strong-armed, because they're repeating a long-held, automatic response they learned in childhood, a response they view as normal and appropriate. In fact, it's such an automatic response that they often don't think anything of it.

This strategy works no matter how powerful or high up your prospect is, because *every one of your prospects answers to someone*, even at the very top: Executive vice presidents answer to the president, the president answers to the CEO, the CEO answers to the chairman, the chairman answers to the firm's bankers and to the board of directors, and the board must answer to the company's stockholders.

2. **Curious Insecurities.** Everyone wants to do well. Everyone wants to get ahead. Everyone is interested in who's up, who's down, who's ahead, who's behind, who's staying even, and who's looking over their shoulder. To varying degrees, each of us is concerned that someone else will pass us by and leave us in the dust. Let's face it: To a certain extent, every one of us looks out for number one.

In short, no matter what their situation, all of your prospects are curious to know where they stand or how they compare with others. Most are also eager to protect their own turf, because they probably worked pretty hard to gain control of it.

When these feelings of insecurity are properly engaged, you can use them to make your prospect *want* to pay attention to your request.

The C.O.L. puts pressure, directly or indirectly, on your prospect's points of greatest insecurity and concern. Because you're coming in from the top down (or, in some cases, sideways), your prospect worries that if they don't let you in their door, they may suffer, while someone else inside or outside the organization benefits. At the same time, your top-down movement through the organization arouses their intense curiosity. They want (often desperately) to know how you got connected at such a high level, who you know up there, and what it might mean for their own professional advancement and security. These are powerful motivators you can use to open your prospect's door.

3. **Competitiveness.** I don't need to explain how competitive many of us can be in our jobs, educations, social lives, families, and hobbies—even in what we wear, where we live, or what our children do after school. Our society as a whole is extremely competitive, and it's not likely to get any less so in the years to come.

Many of your prospects want to be better at their jobs (or at least better rewarded or more acknowledged) than their peers. There is nothing wrong with that. In fact, the stronger a competitor your prospect is, the more leverage you gain to navigate your way in their door.

One of the ways the C.O.L. works is by pitting your prospect against everyone they view as their competition. These people are: (1) others in their organization who hold similar or higher positions, or similar or higher degrees of authority; (2) their immediate subordinates, who are bucking for *their* job some day; and (3) their counterparts at other firms in the industry. Once your prospects realize that *you may already be dealing with their competition*, they absolutely *have* to enter the fray. And their one and only chance to get in the game and win is to let you in their door and hear what you have to say.

4. **The Strong Desire to Be a Serious Player.** Many of your prospects have a fierce desire to be connected, to be in the loop or in the know, to feel that they're important and have something substantial to contribute. They want to be viewed as a major player, a "big hitter." *They want to feel that nothing of importance goes down without their knowledge or approval.* And when they sense that this connection may be taken away from them—when they feel that something potentially important is happening that they don't know about— they *immediately* scramble to catch up with it so they can be in the know again. The C.O.L. works in part by creating a loop that includes your prospect's coworkers, superiors, and/or competitors but *excludes your prospect*. This makes them feel unimportant, irrelevant, and in many cases worried or frightened. Suddenly they feel an intense need to become a part of that loop. And the only way your prospect can get into that loop is by letting you in their door!

For those of you who feel like this process is an attempt to shape, mold, order, guide, and control others' actions, you're correct! It's the basic psychology behind any successful sales, marketing, or persuasion process. *And it's no different from the stimuli we were all taught to respond to since our early childhood—and continue to respond to.* Our parents, siblings, friends, relatives, and business associates all try to get us to respond the way *they* want by using certain techniques; we do the same in return. The C.O.L. is no different.

*Of course, if you believe that all your prospects are mature adults who can make up their own minds based on the naked benefits of your offer, without **any** outside stimuli . . . and that they'll make 100 percent rational decisions, I wish you good luck. Why? Because it runs contrary* *to how we've all learned to behave. Remove the stimuli that we've all grown up responding to, and most people **will not** act or react! That's why the C.O.L. is necessary.*

Remember, the sole purpose of the C.O.L. is to get a face-to-face appointment (or other desired form of access) with each of your prospects. You're not trying to strong-arm or hoodwink anyone into anything. All you're doing is trying to gain access, so that you can present your offer or capabilities.

When to Use the Circle of Leverage System— and When Not To

You can use the C.O.L. in *any* situation where you need to get in someone's door, regardless of who your prospect is. Because every prospecting situation is different, you can custom-tailor the system to suit whatever circumstances you encounter. Therefore, there is literally no situation or circumstance where the proper use of the system is inappropriate or unwarranted.

In other words, it *makes no sense* to use the bottom-up approach sometimes and the C.O.L. other times. The C.O.L. is *always* the most effective way to gain access, regardless of where you're starting from or what you hope to achieve.

But before you use it, you need to understand—in your brain, your heart, and your gut—that it's more than just an effective technique. *It's a new philosophy . . . a whole new way of thinking about how you approach people in order to get access to them.* It is very serious, very personal, very powerful, and very direct. It must be used correctly and wisely, or you do both yourself and your prospect a huge disservice.

Therefore, it should *never* be used carelessly. Before you use it in *any* situation, you must ask yourself—and answer—these questions: Do I have a genuine, rock-solid belief in what I'm offering, and can I provide clear, quantifiable support for it, both to my prospect and to myself? In other words, do I *deserve* to get in my prospect's door?

Whether you're presenting yourself, a product or service, or an idea, if you are not genuinely convinced of its value, then you shouldn't be presenting it. First of all, it's ethically questionable. Second, if you

The Circle of Leverage System

Your Prospect's Fear of Loss	Your Prospect's Curious Insecurities	Your Prospect's Competitiveness	Your Prospect's Desire to Be a Serious Player
• Loss of their job • Loss of possible promotion • Loss of their credibility • Loss of respect from their superiors • Loss of respect from their peers and equals • Loss of power • Loss of authority • Loss of trust • Loss of responsibility	• Who else is involved? • What kind of media exposure is this getting? • Who else is paying attention? • Should I be paying attention myself? • What if this is important?	• Toward competing firms • Toward other divisions or units within their own firm • Toward their equals within their company • Toward subordinates who are bucking for their job	•Within their organization • Within their unit or division • Among their equals and peers • Within their industry • In their boss's eyes

Leverage Point #2
Person inside or outside the company

Leverage Point #1
Person inside or outside the company

Leverage Point #3
Person inside or outside the company

Your Ultimate Prospect

You
Cumulative leverage from Leverage Points motivates your prospect to open their door to you.

don't have a firm, *justified* faith in your offer, it's too easy for your prospects to blow you off course, punch holes in your presentation, and ultimately knock you down on your way in through their door.

I am not talking about holding a pep rally in your head. The C.O.L. is not some rah-rah motivational strategy, or a self-hypnosis tactic for creating the right attitude. Nor am I talking about becoming an ultra–high-pressure pest who won't shut up. I mean this:

- Do you *genuinely* believe that your offer will *significantly* benefit the person or organization you're targeting?

- Can you *clearly* demonstrate those benefits quickly and easily?

- Do you *truly* feel that your offer is superior—or at least equal—to anything else available to that person or organization?

- Can you *support* these personal convictions with real, quantifiable evidence, results, or facts?

Please, no BS here—just serious, honest answers.

One of the central elements that the C.O.L. requires is a rock-solid, quietly secure knowledge that your offer will truly benefit your prospect and/or their organization. Without this confidence, you deserve to be frozen out. Therefore, you must be centered in yourself, genuinely confident that you're not wasting your prospect's time, and secure in the knowledge that what you have to offer will truly help your prospect.

Some Words to the Fainthearted

The Circle of Leverage System will have you calling on levels of people you may not have had much—or any—experience with in the past. That's fine. Please trust the system. It works. If you can't visualize yourself talking with the vice president of operations, chief financial officer, executive vice president, executive director, national buyer or manager, head of a particular unit or facility, or maybe even the president, you need to change your mind-set and your vision. You will be using this system to get into the organizations you are prospecting at high levels. You will find yourself meeting and talking with serious movers and shakers.

Please understand that these are the people you'll be dealing with. Expect it, plan on it, and welcome it. Though you may not realize it now, this change will make your life much easier—and more fun!

In Summary:

- The C.O.L. contains ten Preparation Steps and five Execution Steps, which enable you to surround each of your prospects with the correct kind and amount of leverage.

- In using the C.O.L., you never target only one person in an organization at a time. Instead, you select a prospect, then *also* target two, three, or more other people—called Leverage Points—who influence that prospect.

- By contacting all of these people at once, you flush out your prospect in a top-down pattern. This process creates a funneling effect in which more and more pressure is brought to bear on your prospect.

- The C.O.L. works by triggering your prospect's four Key Engagers: (1) fear of loss; (2) curious insecurities; (3) competitiveness; and (4) strong desire to be a "serious player."

- Before you use the C.O.L., you must have a firm, justified belief in the value of your offer. If you don't, you don't deserve to gain access.

- The C.O.L. will put you in touch with high-level people, so prepare yourself to deal with movers and shakers.

Seven

Pinpoint Your Prospects:
People With the Power
to Say Yes

Think back to the last time you bought a car. You probably did some research, took a few test drives, and eventually decided on the car you wanted. Then you sat down with a salesperson, dickered for a while, and eventually settled on a price.

And did you then sign some papers and drive off?

Not if your experience was typical. In most cases, your salesperson had to get your agreed-upon price approved by their sales manager. And if the sales manager said no, there was no deal, no paperwork, no car—but plenty of frustration.

You probably said to yourself, "Why do I have to go through this nonsense? Why can't I just negotiate with the sales manager? That's the person with the power to say yes or no. If I could deal directly with them from the start, I'd be much better off." And you *would* be much better off—which is precisely why car dealers make sure that's what you don't get to do.

Apply this same principle to your livelihood. In order to get anywhere, you need to get in and make your presentation to *the right person or people*, the ones who have the authority to say yes to your offer. Otherwise you're wasting your time.

Drawing your own circle of leverage therefore begins with *determining who your prospects will be.* This means, first, carefully selecting the organizations you intend to target, and, second, selecting the correct person or people to target within each organization. These are the people on whom you will ultimately bring to bear the full power of the C.O.L.

In most organizations, many different people, at many different levels, are authorized to say no. But precious few are authorized to give a *meaningful* yes that carries with it the power to close deals, cut checks, or hire new employees.

In most midsize or large corporations, there may be six to sixty different people who have the authority to make major decisions, and hundreds who can make significant ones. But there is probably *only one person or group that has the authority to say yes to what you have to offer.* Obviously, you need to know who that person or group is likely to be.

Notice I said "is likely to be," not "is." While sometimes you may know exactly who your prospect is, it's often impossible to nail down in advance exactly who they are. Every organization is unique. The right person at one company might be a level higher or lower than the right person at a competitor. At yet another company the right person might have a completely different title. And at still another, your ultimate prospect might be a committee rather than a person. Your task is to make your best educated guess (based on careful research) about who your prospect is in each organization you approach.

It's essential that you do sufficient background research to determine that:

1. Each organization you target is a likely candidate for what you have to offer, present, or sell.

2. Each person (or group) you target as a prospect either has the power to say yes to your offer or *is closely connected to* the person or group that *does* have that power (i.e., your actual prospect will turn out to be their boss, colleague, or subordinate).

The single biggest mistake people make in using the C.O.L. is targeting the wrong person or people. The only way to avoid this situation is to do some careful and thoughtful research up front.

Another common mistake is approaching the wrong organizations entirely. So, before you begin targeting a particular person or group as a prospect, you need to make sure that:

- The organization can genuinely benefit from your offer.

- The organization can afford it.

- The organization is currently in a position to acquire what you're offering (e.g., it's not embroiled in a merger, a top-to-bottom reorganization, a takeover attempt, a major lawsuit, a criminal indictment, a bankruptcy, etc.).

Here are some of the things to find out about each organization you are thinking of targeting:

1. Full official name of the organization

2. List of all its branches, divisions, units, and/or subsidiaries

3. Address of corporate headquarters, and/or of the branch, division, unit, or subsidiary you intend to approach

4. Main switchboard number

5. Main fax number

6. Web site address

7. Number of employees

8. Description of its primary business(es)—i.e., its main products or services, customers, etc.

9. Description of its secondary business(es)

10. Profits (or losses) for each of the past five years

11. Names of all members of its board of directors

12. Names and titles of all officers of the organization

13. Names, titles, addresses, phone numbers, *and fax numbers* of the organization's (or division's) top executives

14. Names, titles, addresses, phone numbers, *and fax numbers* of appropriate department and/or division heads

15. Names, addresses, phone numbers, and fax numbers of the executive assistants and secretaries to the people in #13 and/or #14

16. Significant corporate events (buyouts, takeovers, reorganizations, major litigation, etc.) in the past one to three years

Don't let this list make you nervous. Often you don't need all of it. And none of it is difficult or time-consuming to obtain. With experience, you'll get more and more efficient at doing research.

Informational Resources

I strongly suggest that as you conduct your research, you prepare an Organization Profile for each company you plan to approach. Photocopy the form on pages 73–75, then complete one for each organization in question.

Below are some excellent sources of information. The specific resources you'll use will depend on the organizations you're researching and the information you need. For any one organization, however, you'll usually need to consult no more than two or three of the resources below. (Typically, I find myself using one of the *Yellow Books* and one or two other sources.)

Yellow Books: These are directories that contain a good deal of basic information on thousands of U.S. organizations. Separate Yellow Books are published in each of the following categories: Corporate, Financial, News Media, Associations, Law Firms, Government Affairs, Congressional, Federal, Federal Regional, State, and Municipal. Yellow Books are available in many libraries, or directly from Leadership

Directories, Inc., 104 Fifth Avenue, New York, NY 10011 (212) 627-4140.

Business Directories:

Business Organizations, Agencies, and Publications Directory
Corporate Technology Directory
Directory of Corporate Affiliations
Directory of Leading Private Companies
Dun's Directory of Service Companies
Encyclopedia of Associations
Metromail Corporation (provides customized directories of information on consumers and companies to help you identify trends, patterns, and prospects)
Million Dollar Directory: Leading Public and Private Companies
Standard & Poor's Register of Corporations, Directors and Executives (Vol. 1: Corporations; Vol. 2: Directors and Executives)
Thomas Register of American Manufacturers
U.S. Industrial Directory
Ward's Business Directory of U.S. Private and Public Companies
Who Owns Whom: North America
Yearbook of International Organizations, Vol. 1: Organization Descriptions and Index

Directories of Management Leaders:

Biographical Directory of American Business Leaders
Reference Book of Corporate Management
Who's Who in America
Who's Who in Finance and Industry

Miscellaneous Directories:

Encyclopedia of Business Information Sources
National Fax Directory

Most of the above items are available in large public and university libraries. Many are also available on disk, CD-ROM, and/or on-line services.

Organization Descriptions: Dun & Bradstreet, Fortune, Hoover's, R. R. Donnelley, and several other organizations publish brief but detailed profiles on many thousands of public and private U.S. and foreign corporations. Some of these focus on basic facts; others include short corporate histories. Several of these organizations also publish supplemental Executive Profiles that provide additional de-

Organization Profile

Name _____

Branches, units, divisions, subsidiaries _____

_____

_____

_____

_____

Address (main headquarters) _____

Main phone (headquarters) _____

Main fax (headquarters) _____

Address (specific division or unit) _____

Main phone (division or unit) _____

Main fax (division or unit) _____

Web site address _____

Number of employees: entire organization _____

division or unit _____

Primary business(es) _____

_____

Secondary business(es) _____

_____

Profit (or loss): last year _____

19_____   _____

19_____   _____

19_____   _____

19_____   _____

Board of directors (names)   Chair: _____

_____

_____

_____

_____

_____

_____

Officers of the corporation

    Title _____ Name _____

    Title _____ Name _____

    Title _____ Name _____

    Title _____ Name _____

    Title _____ Name _____

    Title _____ Name _____

Key executives and their assistants

1.   Title _____ Name _____

    Address _____

    Phone _____ Fax _____

    Assistant's name _____

    Phone _____ Fax _____

2.   Title _____ Name _____

    Address _____

    Phone _____ Fax _____

    Assistant's name _____

    Phone _____ Fax _____

3.   Title _____ Name _____

    Address _____

    Phone _____ Fax _____

    Assistant's name _____

    Phone _____ Fax _____

4.   Title _____ Name _____

    Address _____

    Phone _____ Fax _____

    Assistant's name _____

    Phone _____ Fax _____

5.   Title _____ Name _____

    Address _____

    Phone _____ Fax _____

    Assistant's name _____

    Phone _____ Fax _____

6.   Title _____ Name _____

    Address _____

    Phone _____ Fax _____

    Assistant's name _____

    Phone _____ Fax _____

7. Title _____   Name _____
    Address _____
    Phone _____   Fax _____
    Assistant's name _____
    Phone _____   Fax _____

Other important people and their assistants

8. Title _____   Name _____
    Address _____
    Phone _____   Fax _____
    Assistant's name _____
    Phone _____   Fax _____

9. Title _____   Name _____
    Address _____
    Phone _____   Fax _____
    Assistant's name _____
    Phone _____   Fax _____

10. Title _____   Name _____
    Address _____
    Phone _____   Fax _____
    Assistant's name _____
    Phone _____   Fax _____

11. Title _____   Name _____
    Address _____
    Phone _____   Fax _____
    Assistant's name _____
    Phone _____   Fax _____

Significant corporate events _____
_____
_____

Other information _____
_____
_____
_____
_____
_____
_____
_____

tails on specific key executives. Some publishers of these profiles make them available via on-line services, on CD-ROM, on computer disk, and/or through other nonprint media as well as in hard copy. A handful will also do custom research for an hourly fee.

Public Companies' 10Ks or 10Qs: These are detailed documents that all public companies are required by law to file. The information in these documents is—again, by law—fully available to the public. You can request a copy of a company's 10K or 10Q from its investor relations, public relations, or communications office, or sometimes from its human resources office. 10Ks and 10Qs from large corporations are sometimes also available at large public libraries.

Annual Reports: Issued by individual companies and nonprofit organizations, these are packed with useful information and are usually available by mail at no charge by calling the public relations, communications, or human resources office of the organization in question. Many libraries maintain collections of annual reports from large corporations (either in hard copy or on microfilm). Several on-line services maintain similar collections.

Organizational Charts: These invaluable documents show exactly who holds what positions in an organization and who reports to whom. Most large and midsize corporations guard their organizational charts carefully. Many nonprofit organizations, however, are more open about their structures and reporting relationships. Some publish organizational charts in their annual reports. Contact the public relations or communications office.

Web Sites: A company's Web site often yields a surprising amount of useful information.

On-line search engines: Web browsers such as Netscape can retrieve detailed information from literally millions of sources. Simply type in a single key word or phrase (e.g., the name of an organization or its CEO). America Online, Prodigy, and most other on-line services also maintain their own search services.

Library Fee-based Research Services: The main branches of public libraries in most big cities will do research for you, using knowledgeable staff and a variety of computerized resources, for an hourly fee. In my experience, these services are enormously useful—and great bargains.

Other good sources of information include:

Library Databases: Particularly useful are ones that access recent periodical publications (e.g., InfoTrack). Just type in a company's name, and a list of recent articles about it will emerge. While you're at it, also type in the name of the organization's CEO.

General Business Weeklies and Monthlies such as *Business Week, Barron's, Forbes, Fortune, Inc., Entrepreneur, D&B Reports,* and *Nation's Business.* Most large cities and some states have their own regional business magazines, such as *Corporate Report Minnesota* and *Crain's Chicago Business.* These are widely available at newsstands, libraries, and bookstores that carry magazines.

Trade Journals: These business publications focus on specific fields and industries. These are harder to find, but are usually available at large public and university libraries, as well as some larger newsstands.

Companies' Own Promotional Brochures: If you're not sure what an organization does, offers, or sells, its sales and marketing people will be only too glad to mail you detailed information.

Local, State, and Regional Chambers of Commerce: These are associations of businesspeople whose purpose is to promote local commercial and business interests.

Won't this research take some time? In the beginning, yes. But once you learn where to look, it will take only minutes per organization. I'm serious—*minutes.*

Let me reiterate: You don't need to spend a week, or even a full day, holed up in the library doing FBI-style investigative research on the organizations you plan to approach. *But you must do your homework.* If you are lazy in doing your research, you will likely be shut out. Just think about how you feel when a salesperson gets you on the phone and says, "So what is it that you guys do, anyway?"

The Basics of Targeting

You've done your basic research and know which companies to target. Now you need to determine who is the right person or people to approach at each one. This depends on a variety of factors:

1. The product, service, or idea you have to offer.

2. The cost of your product, service, or idea. (The higher the cost,

the higher up in the organization your prospect will probably need to be. But cost is also relative; a small company may require its CEO's signature in order to authorize a $45,000 expenditure, while a multinational corporation may require only the approval of a midlevel manager, or at most a vice president.)

3. The size of the organization—e.g., its number of employees and/or divisions. (The larger the organization, the more independently its divisions tend to operate, and the more you should treat each division as a separate organization. The smaller the organization, the higher up in the hierarchy you should start out at.)

4. The structure of the specific organization and the way it goes about making decisions. This is difficult to determine through basic research. In many cases you may need to do without an answer to this question until you have made contact with one or more of your Leverage Points.

Depending on the circumstances, some or all of the following may also be relevant:

5. The organization's current position in the marketplace. (Is it the acknowledged leader? Has it been falling behind? Is it gaining market share?)

6. The company's current rate of growth (or shrinkage).

7. What your competitors are doing (who they are targeting, what they are offering, how much they are charging, etc.). If you're not clear about what your competitors are doing, you *must* find out. You cannot position yourself against your competition or make the benefits of what you're offering clear without this information.

8. The time frame in which you must get a response. (In general, the quicker you need a decision, the higher up in the organization you will need to start.)

Once you've done your research, you'll have a pretty good idea of the general level of authority your prospect will have. With experience, you'll get better at knowing intuitively which titles are most likely to be held by your prospect within any organization. The two breakdowns on page 80 are pretty standard.

Zeroing in on Your Prospect

Remember, you are looking for whomever has the power to say yes to you *by offering you a contract, a deal, a job, or, at the very least, a direct and meaningful referral to the real decision maker (your ultimate prospect).*

Here's an example. Suppose you want a job as an entry-level research engineer with BCD Corporation. According to the rules, you're supposed to send a résumé and cover letter to BCD's human resources office. But the HR office doesn't have any power to hire you, only the power to turn you away. (In fact, one of the main tasks of HR offices is to screen people *out.*) You therefore need to ask yourself who *does* have the power to hire you. Answer: the research and development department, of course, since that's the department you'll actually be working in once you're hired. Your prospect, then, will likely be the head of BCD's research and development department. (In general, the person you'll report to once you're hired is often the person who has the real power to hire you.)

But don't automatically jump to this conclusion. Maybe BCD is so large that it has a whole separate research and development unit, which in turn has three separate departments—new product concepts, engineering, and new product development—each of which has a separate director. In this case, the person who most likely has the power to hire you would be the director of the engineering department.

Once you know the title of the person most likely to be your ultimate prospect, you'll probably find their name and phone number in the research you've just done. If not, try one of the other resources listed above, or call the organization's main number and ask.

A Typical Pinpointing Process

Let's go through a sample scenario of pinpointing some likely organizations and prospects.

Typical Structure of a Small Public or Private Corporation

Level 1   Chairman or President or Chief Executive Officer*
Level 2   Executive Vice President
Level 3   Vice Presidents (of various functions and/or divisions)
Level 4   National Directors/Managers
Level 5   Local or Regional Directors/Managers
Level 6   Supervisors
Level 7   Staff (salespeople, administrative staff, customer service, etc.)

Typical Structure of a Large Public or Private Corporation

Level 1	Chairman*		
Level 2	Vice Chairman		
Level 3	Chief Executive Officer*		
Level 4	President* or Chief Operating Officer		
Level 5	Executive VP of _____	Executive VP of _____	Executive VP of _____
Level 6	Senior VP of _____	Senior VP of _____	Senior VP of _____
Level 7	VP of _____	VP of _____	VP of _____
Level 8	Natl. Manager of _____	Natl. Manager of _____	Natl. Manager of _____
Level 9	Director of _____	Director of _____	Director of _____
Level 10	Manager/Buyer of _____	Manager/Buyer of _____	Manager/Buyer of _____
Level 11	Asst. Manager/ Buyer	Asst. Manager/ Buyer	Asst. Manager/ Buyer
Level 12	Local or regional directors/managers		
Level 13	Supervisors		
Level 14	Staff (salespeople, administrative staff, customer service, etc.)		

*In some organizations the top executive may hold two or more titles, e.g., Chairman, President, and Chief Executive Officer.

Let's say you work for an organization called Up With People (as I used to), a wonderful nonprofit organization whose mission is to help build bridges of understanding among peoples of different countries. Up With People provides a multifaceted, real-life, out-of-the-classroom theatrical and cross-cultural learning experience to young people ages eighteen to twenty-five. Up With People maintains five touring casts, which each performs a two-hour, family-oriented musical program. Each cast of 125 people represents roughly fifteen to twenty different countries. The cast and shows travel to hundreds of cities around the world each year; cast members perform for all types of governmental, business, educational, and civic organizations.

Up With People is financed through private and corporate grants, donations, and endowments; the sale of corporate sponsorships; ticket sales; and tuition charged to cast members.

Your job as a regional scheduler is to sell corporate sponsorships. By purchasing such a sponsorship and bringing Up With People to town, a company can do something positive for the city—and its own employees—and generate positive public relations. The average cost of a five-day visit by an Up With People cast to an American city is between $30,000 and $45,000.

Your first assignment is to sell one or more sponsorships totaling $45,000 in the Minneapolis/St. Paul metro area. Because of the size of the area and the number of major corporations headquartered there, you decide to focus first on the largest businesses, those big enough to afford $45,000 sponsorships on their own.

In order to target the right organizations, you go to the Minneapolis and St. Paul Chambers of Commerce and get listings of member companies. Next, you run a Dun & Bradstreet search through the fee-based research service of the downtown Minneapolis library. In this search you request a list of all companies headquartered in the Twin Cities metro area that have annual revenues of $50,000,000 or more, and/or a minimum of 500 employees. For each of these companies, you request some or all of the information needed to fill out an Organization Profile. This research provides you with detailed information on several dozen companies.

Next you get hold of the most recent annual reports for these corporations and scan them carefully. In particular, you pay attention to the letter from the chairman or president in front. You are looking for information on what each company is currently trying to accomplish, and you give top priority to those firms that can best be assisted by an Up With People sponsorship. The annual reports also help you weed out those organizations having financial difficulty, in the midst of a merger or acquisition, or having a poor record of community service or sponsorship.

This enables you to narrow down the number of potential organizations and rank them according to how interested you guess they will be. You also decide to group them by industry—banking, utilities, insurance, media, computers, etc.—so that you can approach the most likely candidates in a variety of different fields.

Next you need to pinpoint your specific prospects. Because you need someone with the power to approve a $45,000 intangible purchase—essentially a purchase of goodwill, visibility, and positive PR—you know you will have to go fairly high up in each organization. From your prospects' point of view, you are essentially selling a public relations vehicle. Therefore, your likely prospect in each company is the Senior Vice President or Executive Vice President of Public Relations or Communications. In firms that do not employ someone with that title, you decide to target the Senior Vice President or Executive Vice President of Marketing, which is closer to public relations than finance, manufacturing, research and development, and so on. You're not absolutely sure that these people will turn out to be your ultimate prospects, but you know you're close—and that you're probably no more than one level (and one reporting relationship) away.

Fortunately, because of how the C.O.L. works, this educated guess is close enough. If you've gone a level or two too high, no problem—your initial communication will get funneled downward, carrying with it plenty of leverage. And if you've gone a level too low, that's okay, too—your real prospect will then be one of the people you've selected as a Leverage Point. As you will see in the chapters to come, the C.O.L. requires you to approach each Leverage Point within your prospect's organization in *exactly* the same way that you approach your prospect. This ensures that your initial communication will quickly flush out your *ultimate* prospect—the real decision maker.

Now let's look at the process of selecting your prospect's specific Leverage Points—the people who will bring pressure to bear on your ultimate prospect by triggering their Key Engagers—so you can begin to create the all-important leverage you need to get in.

In Summary:

- You begin creating your circle of leverage by locating the most likely prospect in each organization you're targeting.

- In order to locate these prospects, you must do some research on the organizations they work for.

- You can do your research most efficiently by using the resources described in this chapter and filling in the Organization Profile forms on pages 73–75.

- To locate your ultimate prospect, you will need to consider some or all of these factors:

  1. The product, service, or idea you have to offer
  2. The cost of it
  3. The size of the organization
  4. The structure and decision-making process of the organization
  5. The organization's current position in the marketplace
  6. The company's current rate of growth
  7. What your competitors are doing
  8. The time frame in which you need a response

- You don't need perfect accuracy in pinpointing your prospects. If you start out a level or two too high, your communication will get funneled down; if you've gone in a level too low, your prospect will be one of the people you've selected as a Leverage Point.

Eight

Identify Your Prospects' Leverage Points

Preparing to Create Your Leverage

Once you have determined who your prospects are, your next step is to locate their Leverage Points. These are the people who will activate one or more of your prospects' Key Engagers:

1. **Their fear of loss**

2. **Their curious insecurities**

3. **Their competitiveness**

4. **Their desire to be a serious player**

Put simply, a Leverage Point is anyone your prospect reveres,

84

fears, competes with, respects, admires, reports to, wants to impress or outdo, desires approval from, or feels a need to keep up with.

When you identify the right Leverage Points and present yourself correctly to each one, your prospect not only feels compelled to give you their time and attention but *wants* to do so in order to feel secure, connected, safe, and in the loop.

Although each situation is unique, a prospect's Leverage Points almost always include (but are not limited to) the following:

1. **Your prospect's immediate superior.** Obviously, your prospect cares a great deal about what their boss thinks—and their boss cares a great deal about what your prospect does on the job. (Even if your prospect is the president or CEO, they still answer to someone—the chairman, the president of the parent company, etc.)

2. **Their superior's immediate superior.** This person's opinion carries even more weight with your prospect, who usually is extremely responsive to that person's praise, criticism, and requests.

3. **If the prospect is part of a decision-making team, other members of that team, especially its leader.** Your prospect sees themselves—at least subconsciously—in competition with other team members. They never want to feel they've been left out of a group decision. Nor will they do anything that would risk a loss of status or acceptance among the group, especially in the mind of its leader.

4. **Their superior's equals in the organization.** For example, if your prospect reports to the Vice President of Manufacturing, other Vice Presidents will usually make excellent Leverage Points. These people can typically bring pressure to bear on both your prospect *and* their boss.

Other potential Leverage Points, depending on your circumstances, may include:

5. **Your prospect's counterparts (people with similar titles and responsibilities) at related divisions or subsidiaries of the same organization.** Your prospect doesn't want to feel left out of something important that a colleague in a similar position is involved in. They fear being left out of the loop. I call this form of leverage *sideways leverage* because it originates at roughly the same level of authority that your prospect wields.

6. **Your prospect's counterparts at competing firms in the same industry or field, whom you approach simultaneously.**

Your prospect has the same fears and concerns about their counterparts among their competition as they do about people in other divisions of their own company. In addition, they are concerned that their competition may gain a new advantage in the marketplace. When you simultaneously approach prospects at two or more competing organizations, *each prospect becomes an additional Leverage Point for all your other prospects.* This is another type of sideways leverage.

7. **Your prospect's *superior's* counterpart—either in another division or subsidiary, or at a competing firm—whom you approach simultaneously.** This person not only represents the competition but also holds a job your prospect may hope to someday land for themselves. As a result, your prospect may be quite interested in what this person is up to. They may also fear being outmaneuvered by this person.

8. **The person three levels directly above your prospect— i.e., their boss's boss's boss.** Although this person is probably somewhat removed from what your prospect does all day, they can nevertheless exert a good deal of indirect leverage on your prospect. For maximum leverage, however, this person should be in the same direct chain of command as your prospect. For example, if you want to get in the door of a company's Associate Director of Retail Marketing, the Vice President of Sales and Distribution can exert considerable leverage on your prospect. The Vice President of Finance and the Vice President of Research and Development will exert less leverage over your prospect, since they are in different chains of command and operate in different realms of responsibilities. As a result, your prospect doesn't care as much about what they think.

Similarly, if you want access to the Midwest Regional Manager of EFG Corporation's Consumer Products division, you'll create plenty of leverage through the Director of the Consumer Products Division but virtually none from the Director of the Industrial Equipment Division.

9. **The media.** If you can generate even a small amount of media attention with your offer—or if you can show that it is already receiving media attention—your prospect will often be more interested in what you have to offer.

On the other hand, the following people do *not* usually make good Leverage Points:

Your prospect's counterpart at another division or subsidiary that deals in largely unrelated products, services, or markets. This person cannot exert any real leverage on your prospect because your prospect is not likely to feel in competition with them. For example, consider the German corporation Bertelsmann, which owns a variety of media companies, including several publishing houses and many music-related businesses. The Director of Marketing for Doubleday, one of its book publishing operations, is likely to feel in close competition with the Director of Marketing for Bantam, another book publisher that Bertelsmann owns. But that same Director of Marketing probably cares very little about what the Director of Marketing for BMG Music Club is doing.

Any of your prospect's subordinates. These people almost never have the power to activate any of your prospect's Key Engagers, even if you have a groundswell of support from some "user group." Furthermore, in most cases attempting to reach someone through a subordinate is nothing more than the old, ineffective bottom-up approach.

As you gain experience using the C.O.L., you'll get better and faster at figuring out exactly who your prospect's best Leverage Points are. Nevertheless, it's virtually impossible to go wrong with what I call the *basic Leverage Point package:*

- *Your prospect's boss*

- *Your prospect's boss's boss*

- *Their counterparts/equals at one to several directly competing organizations (i.e., other prospects).*

I usually begin with this group, then add to it or amend it as circumstances warrant.

Always target at least two to three Leverage Points within your prospect's organization (what I call *internal Leverage Points*) for each prospect. (Three is average, and two is the bare minimum; if you use fewer, your leverage will dissipate much too quickly and easily.) There is nothing wrong with using more, however. In fact, as a general rule, the more resistance you might face, the more Leverage Points you should employ. In those rare cases where you need to pull out all the stops, you may need to use as many as five to ten internal Leverage Points to create the leverage you need.

If you are approaching several organizations at the same time, each prospect automatically becomes an additional Leverage Point for all *other* prospects. I call these people *external Leverage Points*. There is no limit to the number of these you may wish to target simultaneously.

Getting Specific

Return to the example in the previous chapter, in which you want to land a job at BCD Corporation as an entry-level engineer. You've already determined that your prospect at BCD is probably the Director of Engineering. This person's likely internal Leverage Points would be:

- Their immediate superior, the Director of the Research and Development unit.

- Their superior's superior, the Vice President for Research and Manufacturing.

- Their counterparts in two other closely related units of BCD: the Director of New Product Concepts and the Director of New Product Development. Both report directly to the Director of Research and Development, as does your prospect.

- Their counterparts in other companies you're also interested in working for that directly compete with BCD (i.e., other prospects).

Now that you know what job titles these Leverage Points hold, you can determine who these people actually are. The research you've already done will likely tell you. If it doesn't, use one or more of the resources described in Chapter 7.

As you become more experienced at selecting Leverage Points, you'll find yourself doing much of the research simultaneously. In a single thirty-minute session with one of the Yellow Books, for example, you'll likely be able to do research on many competing organizations.

For each company you research, you'll simultaneously gather information on your prospect *and* two or three of their internal Leverage Points. (Remember, many of your prospects will serve as Leverage Points for each other, and people who are internal Leverage Points for one prospect will often be external Leverage Points for others.)

If your research doesn't give you enough information about the chain of command to determine the exact title of a particular Leverage Point, make your best guess, based on your research, common sense, and the charts of typical reporting relationships on page 80.

On page 90 is a diagram of the Circle of Leverage, with space for you to fill in information about your prospect and up to five internal Leverage Points. This diagram provides you with an easy way to keep track of exactly whom you're approaching and who can apply leverage to whom. I suggest you make multiple photocopies of this page, then fill out a separate page for each organization you target. This will give you a clear, vivid, and immediate picture of exactly how you are creating leverage around your prospect.

Hands-On Identification

To get a better sense of how selecting Leverage Points works, let's pick up our Up With People scenario. You'll recall that your job is to sell corporate sponsorships to support an Up With People show in the Minneapolis/St. Paul area. You need to obtain sponsorships totaling a minimum of $45,000 in order to support a visit by one Up With People cast.

So far, you've done the following:

- Decided to focus on the largest companies—those large enough to put up $45,000 on their own

- Obtained a list of all such companies in the Minneapolis/St. Paul area

- Excluded those organizations that seemed least likely or able to sponsor a show

- Researched the remaining organizations

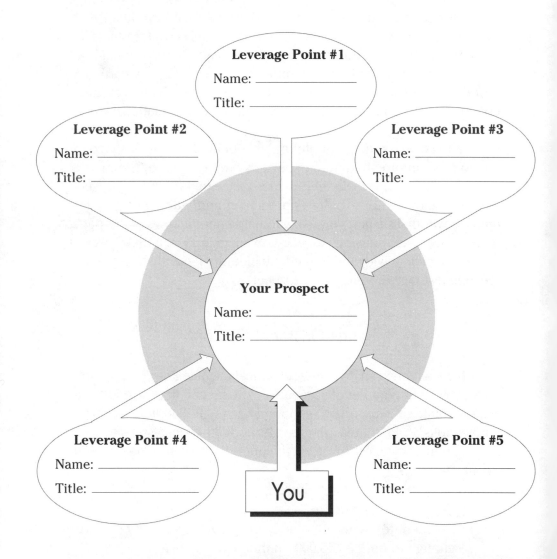

Leverage Point #1

Name: _____

Title: _____

Leverage Point #2

Name: _____

Title: _____

Leverage Point #3

Name: _____

Title: _____

Your Prospect

Name: _____

Title: _____

Leverage Point #4

Name: _____

Title: _____

Leverage Point #5

Name: _____

Title: _____

You

The Leverage You Have Created Gets You in the Door

- Determined that each of your prospects will probably hold one of the following titles:

  > Senior Vice President of Public Relations or Communications

  > Executive Vice President of Public Relations or Communications

  > or, if no such title exists within a company, then

  > Senior Vice President of Marketing

  > Executive Vice President of Marketing

To determine the likely Leverage Points for each prospect, you consult the typical organizational charts on page 80 of this book. Based on this information, plus the guidelines presented earlier in this chapter, you come up with the following Leverage Points:

1. The Chief Operating Officer or President.

2. The Chief Executive Officer. Since sponsoring an Up With People show means putting the name of an organization prominently on display in the community, you figure the CEO will probably want to be involved in the final decision, or at least kept apprised of related developments.

3. For each senior level prospect, the Executive Vice President immediately above them.

4. Each prospect's counterpart/equal in a closely competing organization—if that organization is based (or has a large office) in the Twin Cities. Your prospects in local competing firms will become Leverage Points for one another. Because you are essentially selling local goodwill, visibility, and public relations, people who work for organizations outside of the Minneapolis/St. Paul area won't provide you with much leverage.

5. The immediate superiors of your prospects' counterparts/ equals in competing firms.

With these Leverage Points identified, you go to the Organization Profiles you prepared from your earlier research. The names of virtually all of your prospects *and* all of your Leverage Points appear in these profiles. You make photocopies of the Circle of Leverage diagram on page 90, and fill in one copy for each organization you've targeted.

You've come a long way. You've collected important information, identified your prospects, and chosen their Leverage Points. You may not need to use every one of these Leverage Points—but they're there, ready to use, should you need them.

Now you're ready to make your move.

In Summary:

- A Leverage Point is anyone your prospect reveres, fears, competes with, respects, admires, reports to, wants to impress or outdo, desires approval from, or feels a need to keep up with.

- The most common Leverage Points for any prospect are:

  1. Their boss
  2. Their boss's boss
  3. Other members of their decision-making team (if there is such a team)
  4. Their equals in the organization

- Other possible Leverage Points:

  5. Their counterparts/equals at related divisions or subsidiaries of the same company
  6. Their counterparts at competing firms in the same field (i.e., other prospects)
  7. Their boss's counterparts in other divisions, subsidiaries, and firms

8. Their boss's boss's boss
9. The media

- Leverage Points within a prospect's organization are *internal Leverage Points*; those in competing organizations—including your other prospects—are *external Leverage Points*.

Activate Your Prospects' Key Engagers

Making the Initial Contact

Now the fun starts. In a single simple but carefully orchestrated move, you are about to create enormous amounts of leverage that will quickly and effectively activate your prospects' Key Engagers—causing them to take you and your offer seriously, increasing the probability of their granting you access.

You will make your initial move by sending a simple letter via regular mail, fax, courier, or Express Mail. The specific method you choose will depend on a combination of urgency, cost, and need for visibility. For now, let's keep things simple by assuming that you plan to send your letter by regular mail. (This is what I do most of the time.)

In order to activate your prospects' Key Engagers, however, you *do not* write your usual letter. Instead, your initial communication *must* include all of the following, more or less in the following order:

1. **A list of everyone in your recipient's organization who is receiving the exact same communication.** By letting your prospect know who else you've drawn into your circle of leverage—and by drawing in precisely those people who have the power to reward them, cause them pain, or otherwise influence them—you immediately activate some or all of their Key Engagers. This is your primary tool for building leverage. In essence, you're dropping a cluster bomb, only you're able to determine where each piece of flak falls.

2. **A list of competing organizations whose representatives you intend to meet with as well (i.e., your prospect's external Leverage Points).** Here you create still more leverage by engaging your recipient's fear of losing ground to their competition.

3. **A request for the recipient's assistance in identifying the most appropriate person (or group) within their organization to deal with you and handle your request for access.** This may seem puzzling and unnecessary at first, since you already pretty much know who your ultimate prospect is. However, this request for assistance creates a great deal of interaction among your prospect and their Leverage Points, all on your behalf, which in turn creates strong leverage. *This request is therefore one of the most important parts of your entire communication.* Why? First, it forces communication on your behalf. Second, there's a 50 percent probability they'll disagree on who the most appropriate person or group is. This interaction is exactly what you want. (This request *must* appear at or very near the beginning of your letter.)

4. **A very brief, to-the-point description of what you have to offer and why it is of value to your recipient's organization.** This must include clear, specific, and measurable benefits for your recipient's organization. When appropriate, explain why your offer is different from or better than what anyone else can provide.

5. **A request for a short face-to-face meeting or whatever access you need (e.g., a conference call) and, if possible, some suggested dates and times.** Keep it painless and easy to grant. The briefer a meeting you ask for, the less painful it is for your recipient

to grant. You want your recipient to feel that granting your request is the quickest and easiest way to sweep aside all the anxiety-producing leverage you are bringing to bear on them.

6. **Your stated intention to follow up soon—not only with your recipient, but with everyone else receiving your communication.** Your recipient thus quickly understands that they will not be able to deal with you by ignoring your communication.

Your letter must be no more than two pages—preferably one.

In order to build maximum leverage quickly, it is *essential* that you do the following:

- Send this communication to each prospect, *and* to all of their Leverage Points. Until you connect with your prospect's Leverage Points, you have no leverage.

- Send this communication to all of these people simultaneously. Time your letters to arrive on the same day. If you're sending your letters by fax, send them one right after the other, so they arrive as close to simultaneously as possible.

- Send exactly the same communication to each recipient. Of course, the recipient's name and address, and the list of other people who are receiving the same communication, should be personalized and customized.

A sample of an actual letter (slightly modified for this book) that employs this part of the C.O.L. appears on pages 98–99. (Two more examples appear in Chapter 24.) I used this letter during the summer of 1995 to get in the door of some of the biggest and most prestigious law firms in the United States. I was selling The Power to Get In training seminar and workshop. The letter (and my follow-up calls) did get me in the door of the exact decision makers I had targeted at a number of major law firms.

The specific letter included here is one I sent to prospect Stephen R. Volk, then Senior Partner of a well-known New York City law firm. Let's go through this letter together and see how it makes use of all six of the required elements described above.

Element 1: In the first paragraph I make it clear that I am also sending the same letter to two other people (internal Leverage Points I chose for my prospect): the Managing Partner of the entire law firm, and the Executive Director of Administration, who runs the law firm's day-to-day operations.

Element 2: Also in the first paragraph, as well as in paragraph eight, I make it clear that I plan to meet with people of equal levels of responsibility at several other large Manhattan law firms (external Leverage Points).

Element 3: In the first paragraph I ask for Mr. Volk's assistance in getting me in touch with the right person (whom I believe is probably Mr. Volk himself). Here the request for assistance is implied rather than stated outright—a technique I use fairly often.

Element 4: In the next several paragraphs, I describe my offer and how it will be of specific benefit to Mr. Volk's law firm.

Element 5: In the ninth and tenth paragraphs, I explain exactly what I want from Mr. Volk (a thirty-minute meeting), and when I will be available to meet with him.

Element 6: In paragraph ten, I let him know that I will be following up soon to get his response.

On the surface, this letter may seem quite simple. But in fact, everything about it is very carefully structured. If I had failed to properly introduce any of the six elements listed above, I'd never have been able to develop any serious leverage.

Watching Your Leverage Build

When I teach the C.O.L. in seminars, this is the point where someone usually says, "Wait a minute! I don't get what you're doing. First of all, why are you sending the Leverage Points the exact same letter that you're sending your prospects? Second, do you *really* want to meet with *everybody* you're sending the letter to? Don't you just want to meet with your ultimate prospect? Third, why are you saying in your letter that you don't know who the right person to approach is? Didn't you say earlier that this is one of the most important things to find out? You just did all that research in order to identify who your likely prospects are—and now you're telling everyone that you *don't* know who they are!"

Good insights! But don't forget *you're playing a game*. And at the heart of this apparent contradiction is exactly what makes the C.O.L. so powerful. Despite all your research, *you can't know for sure in every*

July 5, 1995

Stephen R. Volk
Senior Partner
Shearman & Sterling
599 Lexington Avenue
New York, NY 10022-6069

TRANSMITTED BY FACSIMILE TO: 212-XXX-XXXX
RE: GETTING IN THE DOOR OF YOUR DESIRED PROSPECTS
FASTER . . . MORE EFFECTIVELY . . . WITH LESS
EXPENSE

Dear Mr. Volk:

As owner and President of The Boylan Group, I am writing to you, Lee A. Kuntz and P. Douglas Benson, to find out who is the most appropriate person to deal with in regard to scheduling a 30-minute in-person appointment when I'm in New York meeting with other senior partners of some of the city's largest law firms.

Over the past year, I have written a book that will be published by a major publishing house. The book is expected to have broad appeal because of its subject matter, my proven track record, my packaged system, and the power of the testimonials I'll be using . . . a few of whom are some of the most successful entrepreneurs and CEOs in the United States. The book, entitled

THE POWER TO GET IN—A Step-by-Step System to Get in Anyone's Door Faster, More Effectively, with Less Expense

has now been packaged into a training seminar for business executives. Specifically, it is for professionals interested in getting in to see the right person or people, at the right time, so they can deliver the presentation *they* want to deliver, in the manner in which *they* wish to deliver it.

The seminar helps you get in the door of your desired prospects, regardless of your product or service . . .
* *faster than you are now*
* *more effectively (usually higher in the organization)*
* *with much less prospecting expense*

so that you increase revenues and achieve better overall results. The training can also be customized to address specific "get-in-the-door" problems.

I realize you run a highly successful law firm and may feel you have no need for such a service. However, we believe that most businesspeople, from time to time, are blocked from getting at their prospects—and, hence, miss out on significant business. Couple that with the recent pressure on the legal profession to cut costs and increase value, and it's easy to see how the seminar can be of value to you and your firm.

One example that offers proof that my system and the training work in the legal profession is as follows: I recently implemented a custom "get-in-the-door" strategy for a small document-processing company in the litigation support business. Their ultimate prospects were the General Counsels of Fortune 1000 companies. In the past they were rarely able to get an audience with the top lawyer of any of these firms.

However, in the course of four months, using my system, I delivered for this client *seventy-nine face-to-face first-time appointments, each one scheduled and executed.* Each meeting was with the General Counsel and/or Associate General Counsel in charge of litigation. All seventy-nine meetings were with Fortune 1000 companies, including American Express, ITT Corporation, Chase Manhattan Bank, PaineWebber, Chemical Bank, NYNEX, Prudential Insurance, The Equitable, The Travelers, Johnson & Johnson, SmithKline Beecham, Shell Oil, Conoco Oil, and so on.

It seems to me that these are the same types of people and organizations that you wish to work with. My training can deliver more of them to you . . . faster.

I will be in New York next Wednesday through Friday, July 12, 13, and 14, and I expect to meet with the managing partners and executive directors of the ten largest law firms headquartered in New York.

I would be grateful to spend thirty minutes at *most* explaining and showing you how this training seminar can get you in the door of your desired prospects faster, cheaper, and better.

I will follow up shortly with a phone call to your executive assistant to find out if you've seen this letter and if you wish to schedule a thirty-minute time slot that works with your schedule. Therefore, if you would, please let your executive assistant know if you have interest in meeting, so I can schedule a time through them. If you are unavailable, it would still be of value to meet with whoever is second in command.

Thank you for your time. I hope to meet you shortly.

Personal Regards,

Michael A. Boylan
President

situation who the ultimate decision maker in any organization will end up being. You can have a very good idea, but you can't be 100 percent certain *all the time.*

Once your prospect reads your letter, they *can* try to bump you back down to the same low level where the vast majority of people try to make their entrance—*but 90 percent of the time this won't happen.* Why? Because by invoking the names of your prospect's Leverage Points, you've begun to activate their Key Engagers—which means they're worried, anxious, nervous, or at least very concerned about what *might* happen if they *don't* handle you exactly right.

You've activated these Engagers in two ways: first, by letting them know *exactly* who else in their organization is getting the same communication; and, second, by informing them that you'll be making the same offer to their competition—and, thus, perhaps giving their competitors a new and important advantage.

Let's look more closely at how each of your prospects and Leverage Points thinks—and how each is likely to respond to your communication.

Imagine you're one of my prospects, and you've just received and read my letter. The first thing you notice is that *your boss has gotten a copy of the exact same letter.* So has your boss's boss. And so, perhaps, have your counterparts in other divisions—the people who are competing with you within the company for promotion to the next level. And so have your counterparts in competing companies. You have several choices:

You can ignore me or send me away. But you can't help but think that your boss—or, worse, your boss's boss—might call and say, "That letter Boylan sent looks interesting. Why don't you follow up on it?" If that happens and you've already sent me packing, you're going to have some explaining to do.

Worse still, what if you send me away and I wind up helping a competing organization grab some of your company's market share? *You already know* I'm going to your competition, because I've told you that I am. Furthermore, *your boss knows* that I'm going to be contacting (or am already dealing with) your competition as well. And *your boss's boss knows* I'm going to your competition, too. If you freeze me out and I end up helping one or more of your competitors, you just know you're going to get chewed out about it by someone.

Or what if you send me away, but your counterpart in another division of your company gives me the requested appointment—and eventually I wind up helping the company? Your internal competitor gets the credit you could have had, while you earn a reputation for missing the boat.

In short, you're in a jam. If you make the wrong decision here, you could do yourself some damage. Your status could drop in a lot of important people's eyes—people who are very important to you.

So what should you do?

If you're like many people, you'll decide that the safest thing is to grant me the brief appointment I've requested. It's only thirty minutes, and it could save you from some potentially painful consequences. Besides, the offer does sound appealing. This is exactly how many people respond.

You can route my letter to your boss. This takes the burden of responsibility off you, and it's fine with me as well. Now your boss has two of my letters—theirs *and* yours. Your boss then becomes my ultimate prospect, and I simply draw a circle of leverage around *them*—and wind up getting in at an even higher level. And if your boss sends the letter back to you and says, "Handle it," that's fine, too, because you're faced with the same dilemma all over again.

You can discuss the letter with your boss and/or colleagues, and decide among you who is the most appropriate person to handle it. Again, this is just fine from my point of view, for two reasons. (1) I've now caused you and your associates to discuss both my request for access *and* my offer; and (2) that discussion is going to determine who my ultimate prospect is, which helps me zero in on them. And often you'll disagree on who's most appropriate to handle the request. This is good, too—it forces interaction, all on behalf of my request for access.

You can route my letter to a subordinate. If the subordinate genuinely has the clout to make the final decision for or against what I'm offering, then you've simply directed me to the correct prospect. But if *you're* the proper person to make the final decision, your Leverage Points will be watching and expecting you to do the right thing, not pass the buck downward. And because those Leverage Points have gotten copies of the exact same letter—and because you may end up talking to them about it—you won't be able to dodge the responsibility so easily. No matter what, I'm going to stay fairly high up in the organization. I may even wind up right back in your face.

<u>You can grant me the access that I desire.</u> This is starting to look like the only truly safe, smart, and prudent solution, isn't it?

But wait—it gets better.

All of this hand-wringing would naturally occur if everyone knew and agreed that you were my ultimate prospect in your organization—that is, that you were the most appropriate person to handle my request. But in practice things aren't usually that simple. More likely, there will be some uncertainty and confusion and discussion—and possibly some disagreement—all of which will only increase my leverage and the likelihood of your granting my request.

Think about it: You aren't the only person in your organization who got my letter. So did your boss, perhaps your boss's boss, and perhaps some of your counterparts. And I've said that I'll be following up with everyone. Furthermore, you aren't the only person in your organization concerned about where they stand. This means that *most of the people* in your company who got my letter are thinking exactly the same sorts of thoughts you are: "What if sending this guy away would be a big mistake? What am I risking by not letting him in? If I get rid of him, what might I lose? Jeez, look at all the people who know about his request. Everyone who can hurt or help me in this organization is going to be watching what I do."

In short, *everyone* in your organization who receives my letter (except perhaps the person with the highest rank) is concerned about doing the right thing and wondering what the other people who received the letter might do or think.

From my point of view, things keep getting better. Remember, *I've asked every one of my recipients for a meeting—and to help me determine who is the most appropriate person to meet with.* Obviously, it makes no sense for each of you to grant a separate one-on-one appointment. Probably only one of you should meet with me—but the question is, which one? Or maybe a group meeting would make sense, in which case you and your coworkers would have to figure out who should attend, and when. That's hard, so perhaps a single one-to-one meeting would be best after all. Maybe all of you should talk and decide who should respond to me, and how. But you'll have to do that soon, because I have made it clear that I will be following up my letter *with each of you. . . .*

As you can see, I have *forced* my recipients to interact with one another about my request for access in order to sort out who is going to handle my inquiry. That builds still more leverage, *and* gets me an expedient answer.

Remember, this is a game, and the object is to outmaneuver each prospect and their Leverage Points until they grant access. The C.O.L. makes the manuevering easy.

The Power of Percolation

Let's look at this process from an even wider angle. My letter arrives on your desk. Simultaneously, it arrives on the desks of three other people in your organization—people you report to, admire, compete with, etc. All of you read it, and all of you start to consider the request, as well as think through the possible consequences of saying "no, thanks." Almost immediately, the letter begins to *percolate* in the minds and hearts of everyone who received it:

Oh, God, look who else got the same letter. Should I ask Kathy to handle it, or should I handle it myself? Maybe I should talk to Emilio about it first. Or maybe I should call a meeting of everyone who received it—except for Mr. Murray, of course. "Sue, would you call Emilio and find out what he wants to do about this Boylan letter, then let me know, please?" It's probably my responsibility, so maybe I should handle it on my own. But Kathy and Emilio and Mr. Murray have all gotten copies. What if they don't realize it's my responsibility, and one of them tries to handle it first? And if they do handle it, what if they screw it up? Mr. Murray knows they've gotten the letter, and as their superior, the blame will be on me if Kathy or Emilio makes a mistake. I should probably call both of them immediately. Yeah, that makes the most sense—especially since this Boylan is going to be calling us all, and we need to be in synch. Probably the easiest thing to do is just say I'll handle it myself and give this Boylan guy his thirty-minute meeting. But I wonder who should be there. Kathy for sure. Emilio I'm not so sure about. And Mr. Murray—I suppose I should invite him but not schedule it around his calendar. But what if he wants to be there . . . "Sue, would you send an E-mail to Mr. Murray, letting him know that I'll handle this appointment? Tell him I'll schedule it and let him know, so he can attend if he wishes."

And, of course, Kathy and Emilio—and perhaps even Mr. Murray—are thinking their own versions of the same thing.

Now you can see how powerful and effective the C.O.L. can be. With one simple letter, you can get several important people fully engaged with the question of who should deal with you and how— and quite sure that they can't afford to ignore you. This process also helps you determine exactly who your *real* prospect in the organization will turn out to be. As you can see, it flushes them out for you.

Furthermore, in many cases this initial communication alone creates enough leverage to convince your prospect that the best, safest, and most reasonable thing to do is grant you the access you've requested. This way they win, and so do you.

This is only the beginning. What you've seen so far is just the first of five Execution Steps that make up the Circle of Leverage System. The next four steps are more powerful still.

In Summary:

- Your first contact with your prospects and Leverage Points should normally be by letter. This letter may be sent by regular mail, fax, courier, or Express Mail.

- Your initial communication must include:

  1. A list of everyone in your recipient's organization who is receiving the same communication (internal Leverage Points)
  2. A list of competing organizations you intend to meet with as well (external Leverage Points)
  3. A request for assistance in identifying the most appropriate person or group to meet or deal with
  4. A brief, to-the-point description of what you have to offer and why it is of value to your recipient's organization
  5. A request for a short face-to-face meeting, or some other form of access
  6. Your intention to follow up soon, with both your recipient and everyone else who is receiving your communication, to learn their response

- In order to build maximum leverage, you must send the exact same communication to each of your prospects—and to all of their Leverage Points—simultaneously.

- Your communication forces your recipients to interact with each other about your request for access so that they can sort out who is going to handle your inquiry. That builds still more leverage, helping to flush out your ultimate prospect.

Ten

Regulate the Information Flow

As you go through the process of applying leverage, you obviously need to provide your prospects and Leverage Points with a limited amount of information about yourself and your offer. Presenting this information properly—in the right amounts, in the right order, and at the right times—is absolutely crucial if you expect to get in.

It is essential that *you* carefully control this information flow at all times. If you provide too much information, you can destroy much of your leverage—and give people more power to keep you out because you've destroyed the necessity to get together.

Keep in mind these five essential rules:

1. ***Never* send out most or all of your information at the early stages of your attempt to get in—even if people ask for it.** It's an all-too-common scenario: A prospect expresses an interest in meeting with you but says, "Send me whatever information you have,

so I can look it over and familiarize myself with it first. If it looks all right, then we can set up an appointment." You promptly comply with their request. You're thinking, "Fantastic! They're interested." Your prospect then reviews the material quickly, perhaps only half attentively. What they are really doing is looking for a reason—virtually any reason—to say no. And then you get the call: "I've received your information; thanks for sending it. I've had my people review it, and based on their response, I don't see any need to meet right now. But I'll keep it on file, and if we ever have a need for what you're offering, we'll certainly give you a call. . . ." In other words, no thanks, go away.

Giving your prospects and Leverage Points detailed information too soon puts all your leverage in their hands, and makes it far too easy for them to say no without ever meeting with you. So don't do it! It's nothing more than a trap—and if you walk into it, you'll probably get caught.

Once your prospect decides they want to know more about what you're offering, they want to waste as little time as possible. They want *all* the information about your offer, *right now*, up front, so they can make a snap decision about whether or not they want to meet with you.

However, this is *not* what *you* want. You want access—in most cases, a face-to-face appointment—so that you can best present what you have to offer, giving you the best chance to build real rapport. Therefore, to use the C.O.L. properly, you must both supply information to your prospects and Leverage Points *and* withhold it. *You must supply enough information to intrigue them and whet their appetites— but not enough for them to make an informed decision until you've met face to face.*

Put yourself in your prospect's shoes. You're busy, anxious, and stressed out. You want to deal with inquiries from strangers as quickly and expediently as possible. Scheduling and holding a meeting or conference takes time, thought, planning, and energy. In contrast, briefly reviewing some information first sounds much easier. So of course you ask for some material to look over, in the hope that you can make your decision based on that alone. And, though you might not admit it to yourself, subconsciously you're probably looking for a quick and easy way to say "no, thanks," so that you can get back to more pressing matters.

You must respond to all requests for information very carefully.

On the one hand, you must give people *some* of what they ask for—that is, some real and useful information. (*Never* discount or blow off someone's request for information—it's foolish and counterproductive.) On the other hand, you must never, either orally or in writing, give away enough information that your prospect can make an informed decision based on that information alone. You want to lay down a trail of enticing, bite-sized morsels of information that leads your prospect closer and closer to you, until they finally grant your request for access. *Then* you can make the presentation *you* wish to make, in the manner in which *you* wish to make it.

Of course, if a prospect or Leverage Point asks you direct questions about your offer, answer them, at least the more general ones. And when someone asks for material, by all means send some. But *always* hold back the more detailed and important information, and continue to press for the access you need. For example: "I'm happy to put some information in the mail. But to fully understand all the ways our product can increase your productivity and save you money, we should schedule a thirty-minute presentation that works with your schedule."

No matter how much advance information you are asked to supply, keep the amount you provide limited, and feed it to your prospects slowly, one spoonful at a time—until you've gotten in their door.

The one question prospects are most likely to ask at the early stages of your attempt to get in is, "Who else is using this product, service, or concept, or something similar?" Therefore, the most effective information to spoon-feed your prospect at first is a detailed answer to this question—even if they haven't asked it. Since most businesspeople are always concerned about what their competitors are doing, this alone can often create enough leverage to get you your desired access.

2. **In general, avoid making your entire presentation over the phone, on video, or in any manner except in person.** Your prospect may suggest an alternative to a face-to-face meeting, such as an initial video conference or conference call. They may even say, "Why don't you make your presentation to me over the phone right now? You've got me now, so let me have it." Unless your situation or offer clearly demands otherwise, *don't do this*, because it can limit or

destroy any potential rapport that a face-to-face presentation will help you build. Respond with something like this: "I'm glad you're interested in learning more about my offer. My experience is that people get the clearest understanding of the benefits through the in-person presentation. It takes no more than half an hour, and I can do it in your office. I'm trying to make the best use of your time and mine."

What if your prospect absolutely *insists* on an initial electronic conference instead of a flesh-and-blood meeting? In most cases, go ahead with it. But throughout the conference, carefully spoon-feed your prospect information. And, unless your circumstances make a later face-to-face meeting impossible or unnecessary, always withhold at least one or two important pieces of information. Until then, remember, before your prospect says yes to your offer, they will usually want to meet with you face to face—so save those final key pieces of information for that meeting.

3. **Carefully control the content of the information you send to your prospects and Leverage Points.** Do this by breaking down all of your information into separate components—two at the very least, preferably three or four. Then feed these to your prospects and Leverage Points one component at a time, with the final component(s) saved for your actual presentation.

The **first component**—what you'll include in your initial letter— should include the following:

- Basic information that frames and describes your offer *in one sentence or less*.

- The specific, clear, net benefits and outcomes it can deliver to your prospects (and/or their organizations).

- If applicable, the answer to the question, "Who else is using this same product, service, or concept—or something similar?" and the benefits those organizations are reaping from it.

- Some parameters to help your prospects decide for themselves if they might be in the market for what you have to offer— again, in no more than one sentence. For example, "Of the fifteen corporations that have purchased this new system so far, five are companies in your industry of about the same size as your organization." (This last item is optional.)

You must *not* include in this component any real "meat"—technical information, specifications, prices, key documents, etc.

Your **second component** should contain somewhat more specific and detailed information (e.g., a handful of general specifications, possible uses or configurations, etc.). The **third component**, if you have one, can be even more specific and detailed (e.g., it might include price ranges, options, installation schedules, etc.).

If a prospect asks for more information once they've looked over the first component, don't simply agree to send it; instead, press for the access you need. Nevertheless, it is a good idea to have a second—and perhaps even a third—preliminary component available to entice those prospects who are reluctant to grant the appointment. In all cases, however, save your most important and convincing information for your presentation. And always press for the access you need at every stage. *Remember, the more information you release prior to your actual presentation, the more control you lose, the more control your prospect gains, and the smaller your chances of getting in become.* Think about it. What motivation do you give your prospect to meet with you if you send them all the information they want right up front? None!

Be careful, though. You're walking something of a tightrope here. If you play it too casual or drag your feet ("I really can't reveal any details about our wonderful service except in person"), your prospects will simply say, "Forget it; it's not worth playing these games."

One excellent way to keep prospects and Leverage Points interested without showing all of your cards is to lace each information component with a few *credibility bricks*. These are pieces of extremely favorable information scattered throughout your material that you *know* will interest your prospects and keep them alert and engaged. Credibility bricks might include

- Endorsements from people or organizations your prospects and Leverage Points recognize, respect, fear, and/or compete with

110

- Names of customers that your prospects and Leverage Points will find impressive

- Statistics or specifications that demonstrate the merit, effectiveness, or superiority of your offer

- Notable experience that you or your organization have had, including case histories, success stories, etc.

It is essential that each credibility brick relate directly to what is most important to your prospects (and their organizations). Simple boasting, unjustified confidence, or arrogance does nothing for you—and may even turn prospects away.

4. **Control the speed at which you deliver information.** You must carefully control when a prospect receives each information component. If, for instance, you send your first batch of information, and they immediately fax or call you requesting more, *don't* rush eagerly to supply it. Instead, press for the access you need. You may need to dance, sponge, and reiterate (see Chapter 26) until you convince your prospect that it is in their best interest to meet with you. If your prospect still insists on seeing more material first, put more in the mail—but only after waiting three or four days. Then press for access once again.

If your prospect continues to want more and more information before setting up an appointment or conference, they are probably looking for a reason not to see you, a reason to say no. Therefore, by continuing to comply with each request, you're giving your prospect more and more ammunition with which to shoot you down. (Trust me. I've been shot down by falling into this trap hundreds of times.)

5. **Control the "portion size" of the information your prospects and Leverage Points receive.** When you send information via fax or mail, you obviously want it to be looked at, not ignored or put aside—and you want it to be reviewed by the proper person. So package your information in easy-to-review, easy-to-remember sound bites—in sips, not gulps. Use bulleted or numbered lists when possible.

You must treat your prospects and Leverage Points as if they aren't very hungry for your offer, because they usually aren't—no matter how much they may be able to benefit from it. Remember these words: *bite-size chunks.* Give people a chance to digest the information you give them. Never force-feed them. (In fact, many companies' standard brochures contain too much information. The prospect doesn't need to know all that stuff up front. Many brochures give prospects just enough ammunition to say, "There's no need to meet, but thank you.")

Most people funnel lots of information quickly in their prospect's direction. This is exactly what *not* to do. Imagine that you're holding a funnel, with the narrow side down, directly over your prospect's mouth. Now, jam all your information down the funnel. How comfortable do you think they are? Chances are you're choking them!

Now turn the funnel upside down, and imagine that you're holding it above your prospect's cupped hands. Then, one by one, carefully drop easy-to-swallow, easy-to-digest, bite-size chunks of information through the top of the funnel. Let them catch each one and consume it at their own pace. This is a much more sensible way to digest your information. Even if you're responding to a Request for Proposals that requires responses to detailed and complex questions, diagrams, pricing schedules, etc., you can still benefit by structuring your responses into bite-size chunks.

Keep your entire message as brief, concise, and to the point as possible. Letters and faxes should normally be no more than two pages—ideally shorter.

The more you maintain control over the flow of your information, the more you dramatically increase your chances of getting in your prospect's door. Don't forget, your information is like your ammunition. Use it wisely, and don't give it all to your prospects until you're in their door. Instead, use it to draw them toward you. Otherwise, they will use it against you, by denying you access.

In Summary:

- Never send out most or all of your information at the early stages of your attempt to get in, even if people ask for it. Giving your prospects and Leverage Points detailed information too soon makes it much easier for them to say no without ever meeting you.

- Do give people *some* real, useful information, or you'll seem evasive and impolite. But never give away so much that they can make an informed decision based on that information alone.

- Save your most detailed and important information for your presentation.

- In general, avoid making your presentation via video, phone, or any other manner except in person. Your best chance for building rapport is almost always face to face.

- Break down your information into separate components (at least two, preferably three or four). Feed these to your prospects and Leverage Points one component at a time.

- Lace each information component with credibility bricks: pieces of extremely favorable information that you know will interest your prospects and Leverage Points.

- Control the speed at which you deliver information. Don't rush to supply it on people's request.

- Package your information into easy-to-read, easy-to-remember, bite-size chunks. Use bulleted or numbered lists when possible.

- Keep each component brief, concise, and to the point.

- After each information component arrives, press for the access you need.

- The more you control the flow of information, the more you increase your chances of gaining access.

Eleven

The Elements of the Game
You Can't Control

Successful people never spend time on things they can't control. In the next three pages, I'll discuss those elements and events that may affect your ability to get in people's doors that you can do absolutely nothing about. Be aware of them, accept them, put them out of your mind, and focus on the things that you *can* control.

Neither you nor I can control any of the following:

1. **General trends affecting organizations today—downsizing, "right-sizing," reorganizing, mergers, buyouts, lack of leadership, failure to assume responsibility, etc.** The causes of these trends are innumerable: politics, legislation, war, money, desire for power, new technologies, changing demographics, strikes, natural disasters, fear, jealousy, and who knows what else. Any one of these can dramatically alter whole industries, even whole economies, often in

unpredictable ways. Your source of power here lies not in resisting these changes and trends, but in adapting to them as quickly as possible.

2. **Your employer's past or potential mistakes, and the effect they have on your prospect.** You can't prevent other people's mistakes. Maybe your prospect ordered from your company a year ago and was shipped the wrong product or the wrong color, or the product wasn't assembled or installed properly. Embarrassing as it may be, admit to your firm's error if the subject arises.

3. **The personal and professional lives of your prospects and Leverage Points.** You cannot control the mood or situation someone will be in when you contact them. The person you dialed may have just had an argument with their spouse—or just learned that their sister is gravely ill—or just gotten a big promotion.

But if you pay careful attention and *listen*, you can usually hear in someone's voice (or see in their body language) what they're feeling, sometimes even what they're thinking. Part of the Circle of Leverage System is learning how to *really listen* to people, so that you can gauge their moods, concerns, fears, and desires. By paying attention to others rather than blasting ahead with your own spiel, you can begin to learn what they care about and respond to. This will help you immensely in building rapport, in deciding what emotional buttons to push, and in applying your leverage most effectively.

4. **The timeliness of your approach.** The day after you launch your effort to get in a company's door, that corporation may announce record losses and a major series of layoffs. Or, the week before your scheduled appointment with a key executive, she might be called away indefinitely to the company's London office to deal with an emergency.

There is *never* a perfect time for anything. The fact is, unexpected things happen all the time, and the higher up you go within an organization, the more frequently they occur. Many of them are frustrating. Roll with the punches. (The people I know who are best at getting in their prospects' doors are often the ones who have been punched the most!)

You can predict some of these punches, however. You can often be alerted to the possibility of a takeover, downsizing, or merger by properly researching your prospects and their organizations, as I've discussed. A small amount of careful research can enable you to quickly identify those organizations that are undergoing major turmoil, having serious problems, or experiencing massive growth.

Remember, too, that timing and trends can work for you as well as against you. For example, a merger might cause all kinds of stresses in an organization, but it might also suddenly make what you're offering far more desirable—or more affordable.

5. **Your prospect's perception of anyone attempting to gain access.** The first reactions many of your prospects and Leverage Points will have will be based not on what you have to say, but on their prior experience of others who have attempted to get access to them. Some are biased against *anyone* who is trying to get in their door, particularly someone they don't know. To these people, you may (at first) be a pest or an SOB simply because you want access to them.

You simply can't know what other people's first reactions to you are going to be. That's why it's so important to *immediately* get to the point in your initial communication—so that your prospect or Leverage Point has no time to dwell on anything except your message and your request for access.

One of the many benefits of the C.O.L. is that it helps eliminate your prospects' and Leverage Points' biases and expectations. Or, more accurately, it *redirects* their focus *away* from their biases about you, and *toward* their own fears, curious insecurities, competitiveness, and desire to be a major player. Once their Key Engagers have been triggered, they tend to forget their more trivial prejudgments and instead become deeply concerned with far more important issues— such as where they stand in their organizations and how they can stay strong and safe within them.

When it comes to control, the bottom line is this: Take charge of what you can, and let go of the rest.

In Summary:

- Successful people don't spend their time on things they can't control.

- You cannot control any of the following:

* General trends affecting organizations today—downsizing, mergers, lack of leadership, etc.

* The timeliness of your approach

* The personal and professional lives of your prospects and Leverage Points

* Your prospect's schedule

* Your prospect's perception of anyone attempting to gain access

* Your employer's past or potential mistakes, and the effect they have on your prospect

• Forget the things you can't control. Focus on the things you can.

Twelve

The Elements of the Game
You *Can* Control

There are five key elements you *do* have full control over. When you use these elements properly, you greatly increase your ability to get through people's doors.

These elements are:

1. **Your confidence level in the product, service, proposal, or idea you have to offer.** It's basic stuff, but never forget the obvious: Your message, and your own natural enthusiasm in delivering it, are always being judged—often carefully, and usually with some doubt—by your prospects. Whether you're selling something, trying to land a job, or asking for a contribution of money, time, or assistance, your prospect is constantly evaluating your claim and comparing it against how things actually are.

Some people make the mistake of stretching their story. They exaggerate the capabilities of their product or service, puff up their skills and experience a bit, or enlarge the potential benefits of their offer. They think this slight "enhancement" will help put their offer in a more favorable light. They're wrong.

When you exaggerate the benefits of your offer, you increase the likelihood that your prospect will be disappointed. Even slightly inflated claims can set up false expectations in your prospects' minds. When they discover that the reality doesn't match those expectations, they become disenchanted and even upset. That's hardly the situation you want to be in.

You absolutely must tell the truth about what you have to offer. If you don't, you give your prospects the best reason in the world to send you away: an unwillingness to trust or believe you. And *they're right.* If you aren't straight with them, they *shouldn't* believe you, and you deserve to be frozen out.

So why do people make exaggerated claims in the first place? Simple: because they lack confidence about the *actual* merits and benefits of what they are offering.

Confidence is a willingness to tell the truth about what you have to offer—because you know for a fact that it will truly benefit your prospect. To have this confidence, you must first have intimate and detailed knowledge of what you are offering, and you must study your prospect's organization in detail.

You must also be constantly aware of your competitors' offerings and regularly compare them to your own. You need to know clearly— in both your brain and your gut—just how your own offer stacks up, and is superior or unique in at least one important way.

If you don't have an offer that you can proudly say will benefit your prospect, or if you don't feel good about your offer in your gut, it's my belief that you don't deserve to get in your prospect's door.

Here are some of the things you can do to maximize your confidence level:

- Thoroughly understand your offer—how it works, whom and what it affects, what its capabilities and limitations are, and what specific, measurable benefits it can provide.

- Research each organization you plan to target so that you understand what industries it functions in, how it is structured, and what its needs are.

- Bring your offer only to those organizations that can reap substantial benefits from it.

- Constantly analyze your competition and identify those areas in which your offer is superior. If necessary, *redesign what you have* to *make* it superior in at least one important and measurable way.

2. **Your confidence level in yourself.** I know plenty of people who take a pep-rally approach to building their confidence and self-esteem, but don't do a thing to actually become more capable or skilled. They genuinely think that confidence is an attitude you can talk yourself into.

True, confidence is partly an attitude. But it's also a straightforward awareness of your own abilities. Andre Agassi isn't confident of his ability to play tennis because he talked himself into it or attended a motivational seminar. He's confident because he plays tennis extremely well.

When it comes to getting in people's doors, *confidence is nothing more than a centered, surefooted awareness of your ability to help your prospect's organization.* Confidence in yourself and in your offer thus go hand in hand.

3. **The naturalness of your approach.** We've all received calls where the caller is obviously reading from a script, or where they make lame attempts at small talk. Both types of calls strike us as fake and annoying.

An important element of the C.O.L. is to acknowledge all of this fakery for what it is and put it aside. Instead of *pretending* to be sincere, actually *be* up front and honest. Dump the smoke and mirrors! Come right out and tell your prospects and Leverage Points—and their assistants—exactly what you're doing and what you want from them. ("Actually, Celeste, I'm prospecting him. He doesn't know me.") None of this "So how's the weather in your part of the country?" You must avoid leaving the impression that you're trying to schmooze your way in.

Of all the possible approaches you can use, this is the most natural, because it's direct and to the point. Furthermore, it doesn't leave people second-guessing, because you've told them exactly what you want.

The first time I speak with an assistant or secretary, I usually tell them—before they have a chance to ask me what my call is about—that their boss doesn't know me, and that I'm calling to find out if their superior has read my initial communication and wishes to grant my request. Then I ask if they have the time to take my name and phone number and answer a couple of quick questions, so that I don't need to talk to their boss.

People find this clear, up-front, no-nonsense approach very refreshing. They know exactly where they stand, and exactly where I stand. And if part of their job is to be protective of their boss (as it almost always is), they know up front that if they can help me a little bit, I won't try to push past them.

This whole approach creates an atmosphere of honesty and openness from the start. As a result, when I begin to speak about the benefits of what I'm offering, I'm more likely to be perceived as telling the truth.

The bottom line here is to be honest and straightforward—to be yourself. At the very least, you will humanize each situation. Furthermore, your honesty will often disarm and delight the person you're talking with—and, lo and behold, they'll often help you get what you want, rather than fight you all the way.

4. **The level within each organization's hierarchy at which you choose to enter.** As you go through the third Preparation Step of the C.O.L., you will determine the levels of people you intend to approach. Enter too low, and you can get mired in interactions with non–decision makers. Enter too high, and the people you contact may be entirely unconcerned about the specific benefits you can offer their organization. Entering at the right level is crucial to navigating your way in your prospect's door.

As you saw in Chapter 7, once you've done a small amount of careful research, you can make a very good guess about who has the power to pass final judgment on what you have to offer. You can then design your game plan around this person so that you enter the organization either at this level (the level of your prospect) or one to three levels higher (the levels of their internal Leverage Points).

It is always better to aim high rather than too low. It's easy to get politely bumped down within an organization, but it's difficult to get bumped up.

As a rule of thumb, once you've determined your initial prospect within any organization, the Leverage Points you select should be at the same level or up to three levels higher.

5. **The specific strategy you develop to get in the door—and how you execute that strategy.** The very first moves you make—and how you execute them—will determine how successful you will be in getting in someone's door. Those moves are entirely under your control, and they need to be carefully choreographed and executed. *You* pick the vehicle for delivering your letter (mail, fax, courier, etc.). *You* design and prepare that first communication. *You* decide which (and how many) people to target. And *you* determine the timing for each step of your strategy.

The chapters to come will give you the tools to build and customize the most effective strategy for each of your prospects and Leverage Points.

In Summary:

In the game of getting in, you have full control over:

- Your confidence level in the product, service, proposal, or idea you have to offer

- Your confidence level in yourself

- The naturalness of your approach

- The level within each organization's hierarchy at which you choose to enter

- The specific strategy you develop to get in the door—and how you execute that strategy

Thirteen

Your Neglected Ally: The New Breed of Executive Secretary

This chapter is one of the most important in the book. *It will change the way you look at and deal with secretaries, assistants, and other support people*—people who can do a great deal to help or hinder you as you seek access to their superiors.

My focus in this chapter is on executive secretaries (also called executive assistants or administrative assistants), the people who assist business owners, executives, and other high-powered men and women. They can wield almost as much power as the people they work for—and their intelligence, abilities, and actions can make them either formidable opponents or invaluable allies. Nevertheless, everything I say here also applies to the less loftily titled assistants who serve less high-powered bosses.

Many people labor under the misunderstanding that executive secretaries aren't powerful enough to take seriously or deal with respectfully. *This is 100 percent wrong.* First of all, *any* secretary or assistant can be a pivotal point of contact as you seek access to their boss. Second, an executive assistant has at their disposal some or all of these substantial powers:

- They make preliminary judgments on their boss's behalf.

- They determine how high a priority to assign to any communication addressed to their boss.

- They decide which communications their boss actually sees— and which ones never make it to their desk at all. *(An executive secretary who decides you don't deserve to get in can keep your prospect from ever receiving a call, letter, or fax from you.* That makes them an effective blocker, wouldn't you say?)

- They decide how materials addressed to their boss get routed.

- They have a significant say in who gets to see their boss.

- They can speak of you favorably or unfavorably to their boss, based on how honestly and humanely you deal with them.

- They are almost always closely connected to the issues that their boss is concerned with.

- They are usually familiar with their boss's future plans and schedule—sometimes more than their boss is.

- They are very knowledgeable about how their organization works—where the real power centers are, who's in and who's out, how people and ideas move through the organization, how decisions are made, and how things actually get done.

- They can be an invaluable source of information about both their boss and their organization—and they can provide or withhold this information based on how you deal with them.

Executive assistants are not just gatekeepers. They are influences to be reckoned with, and human beings with important jobs to do. The more you understand and empathize with their situation, and the more you can humanize your contact with them, the more success you are likely to have at getting in their bosses' doors.

124

Notice that I didn't say "the more you can dominate them." This chapter is not about domination. It is about *working with* rather than against executive secretaries, so they become your allies instead of your adversaries. It is about dealing with executive assistants as human beings, rather than blockades you need to get past.

A Day in the Life

Envision yourself as a successful executive assistant. You're quite loyal to your boss, perhaps even highly protective of them. You're working at your desk when you get a phone call, the fifteenth of the day. You answer politely, "Murray Goodwin's office. This is Ms. Baker."

"Hi!" the caller says. "This is Connie Famiglio." It's not a name you recognize. "How's the weather in your part of the world?"

You know the weather isn't really what's on the caller's mind. "It's drizzling right now. What is your call regarding?"

"Is Murray in?"

"Yes," you answer, perhaps a bit abruptly.

"May I speak with him, please, for just 180 seconds?"

Ask yourself how you're feeling right now. Your caller hasn't told you what organization she's with or what her call is about. She hasn't explained what she hopes to accomplish in her conversation or why you should grant her request. She's avoided your direct question, pretty much ignored you, and given you some BS about the weather. You're not exactly feeling like inviting her over for dinner so the two of you can become best friends. In fact, you're probably irritated.

Now, multiply that feeling by about twenty more calls a day, five days a week, fifty weeks a year. Would *you* be inclined to help Connie get access to your boss? Or would you be more inclined to protect your boss from her? At the very least, you're going to want to find out a little more about Connie and her motives before you even consider granting her request.

Many prospectors believe it's their job to act like Connie—to blast or BS their way past secretaries and assistants. They're mistaken. For one thing, that strategy rarely works nowadays. For another, it runs counter to three basic principles of the C.O.L.: brevity, courtesy, and honesty.

When it comes to dealing with secretaries and assistants, you must use these three principles to:

- **Disarm** them, by doing the opposite of what they expect.

- **Assist** them, by giving them exactly what they want, when they want it, in the exact order in which they want it.

- **Humanize** the interaction by being 100 percent direct, honest, and straightforward, and by being very clear about exactly what you want.

I can tell you unequivocally, from more than fifteen years of experience in getting in people's doors, that executive secretaries have gotten steadily more difficult to "get by," a trend that is only going to continue. *So stop trying to get by them!*

Strange as it may sound, you don't *need* to get past them. If you deal with them correctly, they will often give you exactly what you want—and you won't need to talk with their bosses directly at all. In fact, as you'll soon see, you don't even *want* to talk to their boss until you're in their door.

*When you use the C.O.L., you never try to bully or BS secretaries. Instead, you **include** them in your strategy of getting in the door. In doing so, you disarm their defense mechanisms, assist them in their jobs, humanize your contact with them, and enlist them as advocates on your behalf.*

The more you acknowledge an assistant's power, the more they tend to relax and become willing to help you. It's a kind of verbal aikido. If you ignore or attempt to breeze past them, they'll feel an instant need to assert their power by getting in your way. But if you acknowledge early on that their job is a vital one and that they're a part of the decision-making process, you will often disarm them and gain their support by making them *feel* powerful and important.

In short, there are brand-new rules for dealing with the new breed of executive secretary. Those rules are what this chapter is all about.

Here's the bottom line: treat all secretaries and assistants with courtesy, consideration, and respect—even if they don't act that way toward you.

Maybe you're thinking, "Oh, I'm never disrespectful of them."

Well, fine. So how many times have you attempted to blow right past them in the hope of speaking to their bosses?

Defining the New Breed

Today's typical executive assistant fits the following profile:

- They take great pride in knowing their boss inside and out—their style, their personality, their likes and dislikes. (And if they *don't* know their boss very well, they'll still act like they do.)

- They know (or feel they know) what their boss needs to see, and what they don't need to see.

- They are very good at what they do and take pride in that ability.

- They hate making mistakes. As a result, they are usually quite wary about allowing access to their boss unless they feel strongly that the person won't waste their boss's time.

- They want to know *everything* about you as quickly as possible—who you are, why you're calling, what you want, etc.—so that they can decide in sixty seconds or less exactly how to handle your request. In a nutshell, they want full control over your actions.

- They are often motivated by the same fears, concerns, and desires as their boss and seek win-win situations for their boss and themselves.

Here is what some top executives have said about their own executive assistants:

Tad Piper, Chairman and CEO, Piper Jaffray, describing Cindy Vincent, his executive secretary of fourteen years: *We can communicate in shorthand. She is able to sort out what she thinks are my priorities, and I agree with her about 99 percent of the time.*

Curt Carlson, Chairman and CEO, Carlson Companies, speaking of Dorris Campbell, his executive assistant of twenty-five years: *I could never begin to do the work I do without her here. She knows how to handle people. I trust and respect her. She is my right-hand person.*

The late Ruth Johnson, owner and CEO of I.C. System, Inc., one of the largest privately held collection agencies in the United States, describing Mavis Panter, her executive assistant of sixteen years: *Mavis has outstanding loyalty. She's more than a secretary; she's a very good friend. We have similar values, standards, and ethics. We work well together professionally as well as personally and complement one another in our working styles and skills. Mavis is always willing to coordinate, organize, assist, arrange, design, and maintain whatever, whenever, or wherever. I can always count on her to help me do my job to the fullest.*

The message comes through loud and clear: The new breed of executive secretary possesses much more control and influence than ever before. If you wish to deal with them effectively, you must come to terms with—and learn to deal with—their new powers, so that they do not control your fate.

Making the Connection

Typically, your first contact with an assistant will be when you follow up your initial communication to their boss. In this conversation, you should do the following:

- Introduce yourself and your organization (if any).

- Remind the assistant of your initial communication to their boss.

- Find out if the assistant has read it and learn what they have done with it (e.g., passed it on to their boss, routed it to someone else, etc.).

- Find out if their boss has received and reviewed the letter and what their response is (e.g., agreed to your request, routed your communication to someone else, etc.).

- Repeat exactly what you want and when you want it (an in-person appointment, a conference call, etc.).

- Schedule this meeting or conference, if possible. (If the secretary can only schedule a tentative appointment, that's fine.)

- If necessary, urge the executive assistant to take further action—e.g., press their boss for a response.

- Explain that you will continue to follow up until you have a response. Any of the following responses is acceptable:

  * granting your request

  * news that your message was routed to someone else (including that person's name, title, and phone number, and the name and phone number of their secretary)

  * a response that their boss has reviewed your message and has decided not to grant your request

These are your goals. Let's look at some strategies for reaching them.

No More Schmoozing

Executive assistants almost instinctively protect their bosses, deflect undesirables, screen and qualify callers, weigh requests, and determine responses. They make decisions on each request, usually within thirty to sixty seconds. They can pass on the request to their boss, route it to someone else, respond to it themselves, file it, or ignore it. *Your job is to make it easy for them to make a decision in your favor—quickly.*

Unfortunately, upon your first contact with any executive assistant, chances are they'll view you as someone who's trying to fast-talk or schmooze them, then try to slide past them to their boss. (This is their natural and automatic response, since fast talk and BS are virtually all they deal with from people they don't know.)

What can you do to change their initial impression into something positive? Simple: Don't hustle them. Do the opposite of what they're expecting: *Give them exactly what they want and need to know—in the exact order they want it—before they can even ask you for it.* This immediately disarms them, and assists them as well.

Most executive assistants are trained to ask some very direct questions of all callers, and the questions almost always come in an exact pattern. Most callers tend to give vague answers or play their cards close to their chests. This only makes executive secretaries suspicious and irritated—and more inclined to shut you out.

So, instead of becoming evasive, provide everything they want— *lead them*. In a pleasant, courteous, and straightforward manner, begin your call by quickly telling them:

- Your name

- Your level of responsibility, if it's impressive (e.g., "I'm in charge of marketing for _____.")

- The organization you are with, if any

- Why you are calling (to find out if their boss reviewed your initial communication, and to learn their response)

- What you want (e.g., a thirty-minute face-to-face appointment with their boss)

- When you want it

- Who else has received the same letter, and that you'll be following up with all of them to learn their responses.

Be focused and concise; the more you run your mouth, the more the assistant perceives you as scared, nervous, or desperate. Get across the above information in no more than thirty to sixty seconds.

This straightforward, no-nonsense, but friendly approach almost always yields positive results. The executive assistant is relieved (and often a little surprised) that they haven't had to pry answers out of you. They appreciate your subtle acknowledgment that they are busy and need to get information from you as quickly and efficiently as possible. Often they are disarmed because you are doing *exactly what they want*: giving them the information they need, in the exact order they need it, so they can decide how to respond to you.

From the executive secretary's point of view, you are being efficient, respectful, and helpful. But notice what else you're doing: You're creating a positive impression *and continuing to control the entire process of information transfer.*

A Detailed Breakdown

Let's go through this whole process in more detail, step by step, so that you can get a gut feeling for how it works. Follow these strategies and guidelines:

- Before you talk with a secretary, find out their full name (call the organization's receptionist or main switchboard). The names of many key executives' assistants may also turn up in your background research.

- Keep your voice even, firm, strong, and natural. Speak a bit slower than you normally do; fast talkers tend to make secretaries nervous. If you sound excited or hyped up, you'll be perceived as a fake.

- Use the secretary's first name, even if they answer the phone, "This is Ms. Chen." This helps establish a rapport—or, at least, a more relaxed tone. (They'll make it clear if they prefer to be addressed by their last name. Then of course honor that request.)

- When referring to their boss, use their first name as well, or their first and last name together ("I'm calling in regard to my letter to Claudia Hagen")—again, unless they make it clear that it's "Ms. Hagen."

- Begin your conversation with, "Hi. Is this [assistant's first name], [boss's name]'s assistant?" I'm amazed at how many people forget to check whether they're talking with the right person. If the person turns out *not* to be their assistant, find out who is; then ask to be transferred to them. (*Don't* leave a message with anyone else. Because of the all-important relationship they have with their boss, it's essential that you actually connect with the executive assistant.) If the assistant is away for an extended period of time (e.g., more than a week or two), find out who their replacement is, and speak to them. *In all cases, you want to deal with the most direct link to your prospect or Leverage Point.*

- Explain in a sentence or two, *without pausing*, who you are, why you're calling, and who else has received your initial communication. Then ask if they have time to take your name and phone number. Here's an example: "Martha, this is Michael Boylan, President of The Boylan Group, based in Minneapolis. I'm calling in regard to the letter I sent to Claudia dated August 7, which you should have received on about the tenth. The same letter was also sent to _____, _____, and _____ [Claudia's internal Leverage Points]. Do you have time to take my name and number, so I can tell you more about what this concerns?" This immediately begins to disarm the assistant, because I've just signaled that I'm going to give her exactly what she wants, in the exact order she wants it, and quickly. More important, however, I've gotten her undivided attention by mentioning some names that mean a great deal to both her and her boss. At this point, unless she's very busy, she'll not only ask for my phone number, but she'll be paying close attention. (If the assistant you speak with tells you they *are* very busy, simply say, "Thank you; I'll call back later," and do so.)

- Recite your name, title, and phone number, and—without pausing—explain very briefly what your initial communication was about *and that you don't need to speak directly to their boss.* Example: "My letter requested a twenty-minute meeting sometime between _____ and _____. I don't need to speak to Claudia at all if you can answer a couple of quick questions. In fact, I'd prefer to take direction from you." This puts the assistant at ease by letting them feel that *they* are in control of the situation. Their instinctive wall of defense begins to come down because they know you're not going to try to push past them. In fact, however, *you* are continuing to control the conversation.

- Without pausing, check on the status of your initial communication by asking the following questions:

  * Did the letter arrive?

  * Has their boss seen it?

132

* Where is it now (i.e., is it on their boss's desk waiting to be read, has it been routed to someone else, did their boss take it with them on a trip, are they talking about it with someone else, etc.)?

- If their boss has not routed your message to someone else, state your goal of getting an answer to your request for access. Then remind the assistant of the leverage you've applied. For instance: "As I mentioned, copies of my letter went out to _____, _____, and _____, and I'll continue following up with those individuals, because I'm looking for the most appropriate people to deal with. I'll await Claudia's response." Explain that you'll follow up with her soon as well if you haven't gotten a response.

- If the assistant tells you that your letter has been routed to someone else, find out that person's name, title, and phone number, and the name and phone number of their secretary. But before you hang up, you *must* find out whether their boss saw the letter and routed it elsewhere, or whether the assistant did the routing and their boss never saw it at all. (This is essential information for creating maximum leverage later.)

- The more information beyond the items described above that you share with an executive secretary, the more leverage you lose. Furthermore, except in rare cases, the secretary doesn't want or need to know any more than these basics. So do *not* go off on a tangent about yourself or your offer. Keep what you say brief and to the point. This is *not* the time for a sales pitch!

- If the assistant can't locate your initial letter, send another copy by fax as soon as possible. Then follow up by phone a few days later.

- If the secretary asks you to send their boss more information about your offer, or asks to schedule a telephone conference between you and their boss in order for them to decide whether to meet with you in person, fine. Send a limited amount of information (as described in Chapter 10) or schedule the call.

Creating Rapport with Secretaries and Assistants

Here are some useful general tips that apply to any phone conversation with a secretary or assistant:

- Always be clear, concise, and to the point. Provide information in quick, easy-to-grasp sound bites.

- *Never* launch into your presentation. Secretaries really don't care.

- Keep your tone firm and strong—but friendly. No cheerleader excitement, please.

- Speak a tad slower than normal.

- Feel free to ask about their boss's plans, schedule, and reaction to your request—but keep your questions simple and straightforward.

- Throughout your conversation, avoid schmoozing—unless the secretary initiates and clearly enjoys it.

- If you hear commotion in the background, or if you hear a phone ring, immediately say, "I'll hold." The assistant will be very grateful for your cooperation—and you win as well, because when they come back on the line, you know you're not competing for their attention.

- If an assistant sounds particularly rushed, busy, or anxious, say, "If this is a bad time, I can call back later." If the answer is yes, call again. This one simple gesture can generate enormous amounts of goodwill. Often they'll be quite grateful, or even feel they owe you a small favor.

- Keep your antennae alert at all times for anything the assistant says or does that may prove useful in dealing with them or their boss. (An assistant's words and behavior often reveal an amazing amount of information about their superior.)

- Be appreciative and respectful of their time.

- Never be afraid to continue calling every two to four days (or at whatever times the assistant suggests) to request a response. You want and are entitled to a straightforward yes, no, or referral to someone else. You are *not* asking for anything unreasonable, and the secretary knows it. In fact, I've often found that the more a boss avoids or delays making a decision, the more sympathetic their assistant becomes to my asking for a response to my request for access. (If you haven't gotten a response after three follow-up calls to the same assistant, however, it's usually time to quit. If someone doesn't respond by the third call, they're not likely to respond at all.)

Secretarial Profiles by Geographic Region

Obviously, every executive secretary or assistant has their own personality and their own unique relationship with their boss. Nevertheless, I have found that, as a *very general rule*, you can expect assistants in different parts of the United States to have different approaches to their jobs. What follows is a quick general breakdown that will help you to fine-tune your expectations and strategy.

There are of course numerous exceptions to every one of these generalities, so please do not take any of these descriptions as absolutes. Also, please understand that these observations are included to help you, not to praise or offend anyone.

East Coasters: These assistants are typically very direct and to the point—often to the point of curtness or coldness. They can sometimes be distant and standoffish, even machine-like. They are usually quite rushed and, thus, interested in finding out very quickly who you are and what you want. East Coast secretaries sometimes seem almost desperate to get you off the phone so they can go back to what they were doing. They are often very protective of their bosses as well. As a general rule, they work the hardest to prevent people from gaining access to their bosses.

Southerners: These executive secretaries are usually polite and cordial, though often a bit formal as well. (In fact, sometimes they can be quite stiff or very concerned about being proper.) They are not usually as rushed as their Eastern counterparts, and often are a bit more sympathetic to your cause. Typically, they are deeply devoted to their bosses, often to the point of reverence. They often refer to their bosses as Mr. or Ms., rather than by their first names. Some of them are very strict about following the rules and going by the book.

Midwesterners: Assistants from this part of the country tend to be friendly, open, and helpful, yet at the same time professional and efficient. Many are willing to go the extra mile to assist you. Midwestern secretaries seem to have the closest, strongest, and friendliest relationships with their bosses.

West Coasters: I have dealt with many excellent and talented West Coast secretaries, yet sometimes assistants on the West Coast are less focused and knowledgeable about their bosses' activities and calendars than assistants from other parts of the country. While they are usually friendly, they sometimes seem unconcerned about the details you want them to communicate to their bosses. Sometimes they know relatively little about the organizations they work for, and they are typically rather casual, sometimes to the point of being scattered: "Wow, you'd like to leave your name? Oh, okay, what is it?" They also seem to care less about etiquette than secretaries from other parts of the country.

As a general rule, executive secretaries in publicly held companies are more knowledgeable about their bosses' likes, dislikes, and schedules than executive assistants in privately held firms.

Again, these are all generalities based on my fifteen years of prospecting experience. Take them as guides, not gospel.

Other Insights on Secretaries and Their Bosses

- In general, the more timid a secretary is about doing something for you (e.g., tentatively scheduling a conference call), the more arrogant and private their boss is likely to be. (The timidity comes from fear that their boss will be angry at them for being cooperative to a caller without their explicit permission.)

- Another sign of a difficult boss is a secretary who instructs you not to address their boss by their first name: "It's *Mr. Sweeney*."

- If a secretary tells you that their boss keeps their own schedule, chances are their boss is a difficult, highly suspicious type, and tough to pin down.

- Typically, the friendliest executive assistants are also the most self-confident—as well as the most willing to offer suggestions about how to influence their bosses. Usually, their bosses are excellent to deal with.

- The friendlier and more self-confident an assistant is, the friendlier and more self-confident their boss is likely to be.

- In general, the more helpful an assistant is to you, the better their relationship with their boss—and the more influence the assistant has.

Now you've seen how each of the key elements behind the C.O.L. works. It's time to put all of these elements together into a single fluid, step-by-step process.

In the chapters to come, I'll lead you through the C.O.L.'s ten Preparation Steps and five Execution Steps. As we walk through each step, you'll learn exactly how to apply the principles of the C.O.L. in a wide variety of situations, so that you can generate the maximum possible leverage to get in.

In Summary:

- Secretaries and assistants—particularly executive assistants— can wield almost as much power as the people they work for. This can make them formidable opponents—or invaluable allies.

- A secretary can be a pivotal point of contact as you seek access to their boss. Understand and empathize with a secretary's situation and you are more likely to get in their boss's door.

- Treat assistants as human beings, not blockades to get past. Approach them with courtesy, consideration, and respect.

- Never try to blast, bully, or schmooze your way past assistants.

In fact, stop trying to get by them at all. Instead, *include* them in your strategy of getting in the door.

• Assistants want to know *everything* about you as quickly as possible so they can quickly decide how to handle your request. Make it easy for them to make quick decisions in your favor. Give them all the information they want immediately—before they even have a chance to ask for it.

• When dealing with assistants, follow these three principles:

1. **Disarm** them by doing the opposite of what they expect.
2. **Assist** them by giving them exactly what they want, when they want it, in the exact order in which they want it.
3. **Humanize** the interaction by being 100 percent honest, direct, straightforward, and clear about what you want.

• If you deal with assistants correctly, they will often give you exactly what you want.

THE CIRCLE OF LEVERAGE SYSTEM: THE TEN PREPARATION STEPS

Fourteen

Preparation Step #1:
Define What You Need vs.
What You Want

What you *want* and what you *need* are two very different things. If you sell sophisticated technical equipment for a living, you may *want* an hour-long in-person meeting to demonstrate how your product works and the dozens of ways it can benefit your prospect. But is a full hour truly necessary? In most cases, your prospect only needs a mini-overview in your initial meeting, not your entire blast. Therefore, you may only *need* twenty minutes to explain the key reasons why your product is best.

If you're competing for a job, you may *want* an hour or more with each person on the hiring committee, so that you can explain to each one the different ways you can add value to their organization. But you don't *need* all that time—or multiple meetings—to get across to the committee all the benefits of hiring you.

Another example: You're working to schedule an appointment

with the owners of a company, both of whom are interested in talking with you. One is in Boston, the other in London. You *want* a face-to-face meeting with both of them when you're in Boston next week, but the British owner won't be in the United States for another two months. Does it really make sense to wait for a three-way, in-person meeting? Wouldn't a face-to-face meeting next week with the American owner, followed by a three-way video conference a few days later, be better?

Regardless of your product, service, or abilities, in most cases you don't need to (and should not) machine-gun your prospect with a lengthy presentation during your first meeting or conference. Ask for something brief so it's easy and painless for your prospect to grant.

Put yourself in your prospect's place. Imagine someone is asking you for a one-hour appointment. You *want* to let them in your door, but you don't really have an hour to spare. In fact, their request for a full hour annoys you. You're wondering why they need so much time.

Meanwhile, someone else selling a similar product asks for a twenty-minute meeting.

Which appointment are you more likely to grant?

The first step in using the C.O.L. is identifying what you genuinely *need* from each of your prospects in order to adequately present your offer. *The more you ask for, the more painful it will be for your prospect to grant, and the less likely you are to get the access you need.* So don't throw boulders in your own path—ask only for what you need, and no more. This could mean restructuring the nature of your initial presentation. (Believe me: If your initial presentation gets your prospect interested, you'll have the chance to give a longer and more detailed spiel.)

Take a close, hard look at your offer and how and when you plan to present it. How much time do you *really* need to communicate the major benefits? Do you *genuinely* need a face-to-face meeting with all three division heads, or is one enough?

What you need will be different in each unique situation, of course, and will depend on some or all of the following:

- Where your prospect is located

- The complexities involved in properly presenting your offer

- The cost of your product or service

- The expense of making your presentation

- How much you have to gain if your prospect accepts your offer

- The degree and sophistication of your competition

- The prospecting procedures and norms in your company or industry

- The timing of your approach (how quickly your prospect needs to make a decision, or how close they are to making a decision when you first approach them)

This last item alone can make a huge difference—which is why it's often important to find out as quickly as possible if your prospect is in the beginning, middle, or final stages of considering your type of product or service.

Remember, your prospect will follow the path of least resistance 95 percent of the time. So if you can make it simple and painless to let you in, your prospect will be more inclined to grant the access you need.

In Summary:

- What you want and what you need are two very different things. Decide what you need Is it a face-to-face meeting, or will a video conference work? How much time do you really need to adequately present your offer?

- In using the C.O.L., you must make it easy and painless for your prospect to grant your request.

- The first step in using the C.O.L. is identifying what you genuinely need (rather than want) from each of your prospects in order to adequately present your offer to them.

- Ask only for what you need and no more.

- The more you ask for, the more difficult it will be for your prospect to grant your request—and the less likely you are to get in.

Preparation Step #2:
Do Your Homework: Use the
Leverage of Research

Put yourself in your prospect's position once more. Someone you don't know has gotten past the switchboard and your assistant, and has you on the line at this very moment. You're a bit irritated that he got through, but he sounds pretty sharp. He's got no referral or business acquaintance or prior relationship, but he's doing everything right. He's asked for permission to speak with you for only two minutes. He's very clear and precise about why he's calling and what he wants. He sounds like he knows what he's talking about, and he's very professional and polished. He's beginning to engage you, and you're starting to get impressed. In fact, you're saying to yourself, "This guy could give our own salespeople some good advice." So you talk to him for two minutes—and then he pauses and asks, "So what business are you people in, anyway?"

Wrong question! End of phone call.

Smooth as he was, that caller deserved to be hung up on. If he didn't even know what line of business you're in, how could he possibly know whether his offer could benefit you? He proved himself not only lazy, but disrespectful of your time and authority.

Do you want your own prospects to view you this way? Of course not!

Your prospects are not responsible for educating you about their business—you are. You *must* get the facts about each organization you target. Without a knowledge base, you irritate people and waste their time. It's like going into battle with a gun but no ammunition.

The more knowledge you have about your prospect, their Leverage Points, and their organization, the faster and better your opportunity for rapport. Why? Because when you're knowledgeable, you communicate loudly and clearly that you're serious about wanting access; that you've invested some time, effort, and money in trying to reach them; that you're not lazy; that it makes a difference to you who they are and what their organization does; and, most of all, that *you're trying to be a good steward of their time.*

Furthermore, you immediately separate yourself from almost everyone else who is seeking the same access—both in the knowledge you have and in the confidence and leverage this knowledge gives you.

When you demonstrate that you've done your homework, people are usually surprised and impressed. They appreciate the care and effort you've put in and, as a result, are much more likely to open up to you. Often they will also be friendlier, more polite, more willing to listen, and more generous with their time.

Here's the bottom line: When you do some basic research, you stand a *much* better chance of getting the access you need.

Background Research Basics

You don't need to know what color an organization's logo is or what kind of car the CEO drives. But you should know the basics.

In doing your basic background research, you will need to find out most or all of the following:

1. Full official name of the organization

2. List of all its branches, divisions, units, and/or subsidiaries

3. Address of corporate headquarters, and/or of the branch, division, unit, or subsidiary you intend to approach

4. Main switchboard number

5. Main fax number

6. Web site address

7. Number of employees

8. Description of its primary business(es)—its main products or services, customers, etc.

9. Description of its secondary business(es)

10. Profits (or losses) for each of the past five years

11. Names of all members of its board of directors

12. Names and titles of all officers of the organization

13. Names, titles, addresses, phone numbers, *and fax numbers* of the organization's (or division's) top executives

14. Names, titles, addresses, phone numbers, *and fax numbers* of the appropriate department and/or division heads

15. Names, addresses, phone numbers, and fax numbers of the executive assistants and secretaries to the people in #13 and/or #14

16. Significant corporate events (buyouts, takeovers, reorganizations, major litigation, etc.) in the past one to three years

This may seem like a lot of information, but you don't need a Ph.D. to find it. It's actually quite easy once you know where to look. With experience, acquiring this information on thirty companies might take a couple of hours at most.

However, you *must* do your homework for *each and every* prospecting situation. There is no excuse not to. If you don't, and you end up getting frozen out because you didn't know your prospect or their organization, you have only yourself to blame.

Chapter 7 provides a complete list of the most valuable resources for researching organizations. Use them! In addition, in that chapter you'll find an Organization Profile form. Make a few dozen photocopies of this form and, as you do your research, fill one out for each organization you are thinking of prospecting. This will give you everything you need right at your fingertips as you proceed through the steps of the C.O.L.

Remember, before you use the C.O.L. to approach any organization, you first need to make sure that:

- The organization can genuinely benefit from your offer

- The organization can afford what you're offering

- The organization is in a position to acquire what you offer (i.e., it's not involved in a merger, major reorganization, bankruptcy, etc.)

Research Tips and Time-Savers

- The fact is that you can find *any* information you want if you know where to look. More than one hundred companies are in the business of collecting, storing, and selling the kinds of information I'm talking about, and it's available in many formats: hard copy, floppy disk, CD-ROM, electronic transfer, etc.

- If you *don't* know where to look, ask a reference librarian for help. If they can't locate what you need, talk to the director of research.

- I strongly suggest you build a relationship with the director of research at the largest public library in your area. This person can be your adviser, helper, and "digger"—and can save you enormous amounts of time and energy. A good research director can custom-design any type of research you need—the number of cellular phones sold in California in 1993, or the growth rate of single-parent households in the United States between 1949 and 1995, or the names of the art directors of the twenty biggest U.S. software publishers. Research directors usually charge by the hour for their services, but their knowledge, expertise, and skills are well worth the expense.

- Virtually all businesses are categorized by the Standard Industrial Classification code, or SIC. This code tells you the general line of business an organization is in—physical fitness centers, catering services, etc. Your library will have this list, called the Standard Industrial Classification Numeric Listing, in either book or electronic form. Want to get a quick list of potential organizations to prospect? Ask the reference librarian or research director to run a printout of all the organizations in a particular locale that share the same SIC code.

- Be sure to check out organizations' Web sites, which can supply a great deal of useful information. Often specific departments, divisions, and subsidiaries—as well as individual prospects and Leverage Points—have their own Web pages.

- Information on publicly held companies is generally easier and less expensive to obtain than information on privately held firms.

- For every public company you're considering, get your hands on its most recent annual report. (Some private companies publish annual reports as well.) This one document provides most of the basics you need. Call the firm's public relations, communications, or human resources department, or check the largest library in your area. Annual reports are always free.

- If a private company doesn't publish an annual report, ask for its annual review—or, if this isn't available, whatever general marketing and promotional material it has. Contact the public relations or communications department; if that doesn't work, try the marketing department.

- You'll usually need to consult no more than two or three resources to get everything you need on any particular organization. (Most of the time I use *The Yellow Book* and one or two other resources.)

- Most useful resources: (1) Dun & Bradstreet's Organizational Profiles; (2) *The Yellow Book* (publicly held companies); (3) annual reports/reviews.

- Once you're proficient at doing research, you'll average five to ten minutes per company to collect the information you need.

- Remember: *You can never have too much information.*

In Summary:

- Your prospects are not responsible for educating you about their business. *You* are!

- When you do some basic background research, you immediately separate yourself from others who are also seeking access, and you stand a much better chance of getting in.

- The more knowledge you have about your prospect, their business, and their Leverage Points, the faster and better your opportunity for rapport.

- Before you use the C.O.L. on any organization, be sure that it can truly benefit from your offer, that it can afford your offer, and that it is in a position to acquire it.

- Use the Organization Profile forms on pages 73–75 to keep all prospecting information you need easily accessible.

- The director of research at a major library can be your best adviser, helper, and research assistant.

Sixteen

Preparation Step #3:
Decide Who to Target

Now it's time to locate your most likely prospect(s) at each of the organizations you've targeted. While you often can't know for certain exactly who this will be, you can make a very good educated guess. As long as this guess comes reasonably close, the leverage you apply will be effective.

You can zero in on your prospect by finding out the answer to one of two questions. If you are initiating the process—i.e., if the organization hasn't begun a formal search for what you're offering—then the question to ask is, *Who has the level of authority to say yes to my offer?* This is the approach we took back in Chapter 7, and the one you'll find yourself taking most of the time.

In certain circumstances, however, the organization may have already begun a search—i.e., it has put out a call for proposals or job candidates. Then the question you must answer is, *Who is carrying the ball?*

Who Has the Right Level of Authority?

The answer to this question is different for each organization and depends on the following factors:

- The product, service, or idea you're offering.

- The cost of your offer. The higher the cost, the higher in the organization your ultimate prospect is likely to be.

- The size of the organization. (In large organizations with multiple divisions, branches, or units, treat each unit as a separate entity.) The smaller the organization, the higher up your prospect will probably be.

- The structure of the organization.

- The organization's current position in the marketplace. An organization that is very concerned with gaining market share may be more receptive to what you have to offer.

- The organization's current rate of growth. A company with a mandate to grow aggressively or increase its visibility may be more open to your offer.

- What your competition is doing.

- The time frame in which you must get a response. In general, the sooner you need a decision, or the quicker the organization needs to make it, the higher up in the organization you will need to go.

In general it's better to err by going in too high than too low. Starting out too high typically results in a referral downward—a referral that provides the leverage of someone in authority. But it is a mistake to automatically start out at or near the top. *You must stay within the general realm in which your prospect is likely to work.* Never start out more than two—or at most three—levels above where you think the ultimate decision maker is likely to be.

Who Is Carrying the Ball?

If a selection process is already underway when you enter the game—i.e., you've heard about it from an advertisement, a Request for Proposals, or a referral—then before you do anything else, you need to find out exactly where in the process the organization is and what people are currently involved.

How do you find out? Call and ask. Start with whatever name, address, and/or phone number you were given in the ad, Request for Proposals, or referral. Remember, you don't have to talk to the person who heads the process. In fact, once you've found out this person's name and phone number, *don't* call them. Instead, call their assistant. Most assistants are happy to answer your questions—especially when you follow the advice in Chapter 13 and tell them, quickly, who you are, what you want, why you want it, and that you don't need to speak with their boss.

Why is knowing who is carrying the ball so important? Because if you don't, you run the risk of applying all your leverage in the wrong places and blowing your opportunity to get in.

Imagine you've just learned about a job opening that you're extremely qualified for. The organization has advertised the position and is well into the process of selecting a candidate. The human resources department is no longer accepting résumés, has narrowed the selection to four potential candidates, and has made its recommendation to the division vice president, who will make the final decision. Do you apply as much leverage as possible to the people in the HR department, trying to get them to consider you as a candidate? Of course not! You're tackling people who aren't carrying the ball anymore. The vice president is your prospect. (Their likely Leverage Points include the president of the division and the people they both answer to at corporate headquarters.)

Another consideration: The further along in the decision-making process an organization is when you first enter the game, the higher up you will probably need to begin. This is because it's too easy for people lower down in the hierarchy to say, "Although you have great credentials, we've already narrowed the field to three candidates. And we feel we've thoroughly considered all the possibilities, so we don't wish to reopen the process. We're comfortable with what we've done." *That's* when you need to aim high, engage someone higher up in the organization, and get them to say, "Wait a minute, folks. We know the process is pretty far along, but our goal isn't to have a nice, smooth process—it's to make the decision that will add the most value to the organization. If this person looks like they can offer a better package than the others, at least let them make their presentation."

What if, for whatever reason, you simply can't find out who is carrying the ball right now? Follow the advice in the previous section and make your best educated guess about who your prospect is. Then, to play it safe, target the person *one level higher* as your initial prospect.

The key here is to aim high *when necessary*—but *not as a general principle*. In the early stages of an organization's information gathering and decision making, for example, there's usually no need to aim higher than normal.

People new to the C.O.L. often make the mistake of trying to torpedo in at a very high level early in the decision-making process. But if the organization is in the early stages of assessing its needs, it may be weeks or months before anyone is ready to consider any offers. Suddenly the neophyte comes blasting into the president's office, looking for an appointment. They've launched a scud missile when all they needed was a reconnaissance plane to take pictures and gather information. As a result, they blow their opportunity to get in.

Honing in on Your Prospect's Leverage Points

Now that you've identified your most likely prospect(s) in each organization, it's time to determine those prospects' Leverage Points.

You'll recall that a Leverage Point is anyone your prospect reveres, fears, competes with, respects, admires, wants to impress or outdo, desires approval from, or feels a need to keep up with. Leverage Points are the people whose interactions with your prospect will activate one or more of their Key Engagers: (1) their fear of loss; (2)

their curious insecurities; (3) their competitiveness; and (4) their desire to be a serious player. Most or all of your prospect's internal Leverage Points will usually appear in the Organization Profile you've put together for their firm.

Here is a quick list of typical Leverage Points:

Basic Leverage Points

- Your prospect's boss

- Your prospect's boss's boss

- Their counterparts in directly competing organizations

Other Common Leverage Points

- Other members of the decision-making team (particularly its leader)

- Your prospect's equals in the organization

- Their counterparts in other divisions or units of the same organization

- Your prospect's boss's counterparts in competing organizations and/or other divisions of the same organization

Less Common Leverage Points (useful in some situations)

- The person three levels above your prospect—their boss's boss's boss

- Media attention for your offer (or for a problem your offer addresses)

Detailed descriptions of the different types of Leverage Points and how they influence your prospect appear in Chapter 8.

Drawing the Circle

On the next page is a Circle of Leverage diagram—the same one that appeared on page 90. Feel free to make as many photocopies of this page as you wish.

Once you've chosen your prospects and Leverage Points, fill out a separate diagram for each targeted organization. Include as many internal Leverage Points as you feel are appropriate. If you're using two or three, leave some spaces blank; if you're using more than five (rare, but not unheard of), write in additional information as necessary. I suggest that you make the highest-ranking person Leverage Point #1, the next-highest Leverage Point #2, and so on.

This diagram will not only help you keep track of who's who, but it also will give you a vivid picture of exactly how to apply leverage to navigate your way in your prospect's door.

Once you have this picture firmly in mind, turn it into a movie. Step by step, visualize how your initial letter, fax, or other communication will be received and processed by each of these people. Imagine each one reading it and letting it percolate in their mind. Then watch as each of your Leverage Points interacts with your prospect, applying leverage one by one. Finally, visualize your prospect facing the combined leverage of all of these interactions—and deciding to grant you the access you've requested.

In Summary:

- If an organization is not involved in an official search for what you're offering, you can locate your prospect by finding out who has the level of authority to say yes.

- If the organization has already begun such a search, find out who is carrying the ball.

- The further along an organization is in its decision-making process, the higher up you will probably need to enter.

- Stay within the general realm in which your prospect works.

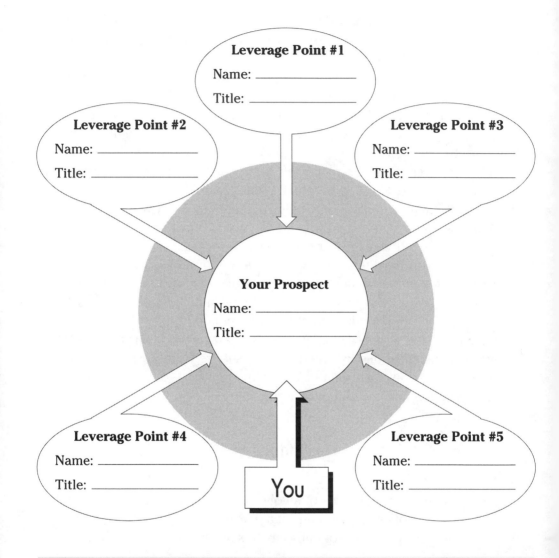

The Leverage You Have Created Gets You in the Door

Never start out more than two or three levels higher than where you think your ultimate prospect is.

- Many of your prospect's internal Leverage Points will appear in their firm's Organization Profile.

- Use the diagram on page 156 to keep track of each prospect and their internal Leverage Points. This will help you visualize exactly how leverage will be applied to each prospect.

Seventeen

Preparation Step #4:
Understand Your Prospect's Nature

S uccess is always easier to achieve when you can first walk in your prospect's shoes.

This step is all about getting inside your prospect's life.

The more you can envision your prospect's world, the more accurately you can predict how they will act. This can help you considerably in your quest for access—and prevent you from being blind-sided by a sudden surprise move.

How can you get inside the head of a stranger? I'll show you.

First, look carefully at the Organization Profile for the company where your prospect works. If you have an organizational chart, look at that as well. Whom does your prospect have power over? Who has power over them? Are they a big fish in a small pond, a medium-size fish in a huge pond, etc.? Do they have more than one assistant—or any assistant at all? What part of the country do they live in? (The geographic profiles of executive secretaries in Chapter 13 apply to some degree to bosses as well.)

If your prospect is a business owner or key executive, some personal information about them may have shown up in your research—age, annual salary, marital status, income, amount of company stock owned, number of years with the company, college(s) attended and degree(s) received, etc. Study this information carefully. It will begin to create a picture of who they are and what they might care about.

If you know your prospect's job title and some information about the organization they work for, you should be able to make a highly educated guess about their duties and responsibilities. Do they work mostly with people, things, numbers, or concepts? Does their job involve a wide range of tasks or the same ones over and over? How much outside contact do they have? How much traveling do they do? Are they under great or moderate stress? Do they make frequent decisions? Is their industry, organization, or profession changing unusually quickly?

Next, make use of your visioning skills. Picture your prospect at the beginning of a typical working day. Whom do they meet with? What tasks must they perform? What are they likely to be concerned about? What people, situations, or tasks worry them?

Follow your prospect through this entire imaginary day, and observe what challenges, problems, and issues they face. Then ask yourself: What is likely to motivate this person—fear, anxiety, admiration, gratitude? How can I structure my offer and my request for access to appeal to their most important needs and desires?

Maybe this exercise sounds too touchy-feely or speculative for your taste. Trust me—it works. While it can't be 100 percent accurate, it does put you in your prospect's shoes and helps you see things from their perspective. Think of it not as a mental exercise but as a form of subjective information gathering. Furthermore, a significant percentage of the time your guesses will be right on the money!

Painting Your Prospect's Portrait

Take the objective information about your prospect in your Organization Profile (and other research) and combine it with the sub-

Prospect Portrait

Name _____ Title _____

Company _____

Division/unit/subsidiary _____

Job description/duties _____

_____

Address _____

Phone _____ Fax _____

E-mail _____ Web site _____

Name/title of prospect's superior _____

Assistant's name _____ Phone _____

Fax _____ E-mail _____

Prospect's sex ___ Age ___ Marital status ___ Annual salary _____

Amount of power within organization/division _____

Number of years in organization _____ in position _____

Prior position and company _____

General temperament _____

What motivates them? _____

_____

What's important to them? _____

_____

Character traits that may help me get in _____

_____

Character traits that may hinder my getting in _____

_____

Other relevant information _____

_____

jective information from your prospect's imaginary day. Then fill out a Prospect Portrait.

The Prospect Portrait is a brief, one-page breakdown of key information. It contains both hard facts and your own best judgments about your prospect.

A blank Prospect Portrait appears on page 160. I suggest making several dozen photocopies so you have blank forms on hand.

You may want to fill out a form for each of your prospect's internal Leverage Points as well. This isn't necessary, but the more you know about everyone you approach, the more you can anticipate how they will respond—and the better your chances of getting in.

It Takes Access to Get Access

No matter who your prospects and Leverage Points are, or what their lives are like, one thing is virtually certain: They are busy. They aren't going to spend their time or money trying to get in touch with you, even if your offer sounds fabulous. So use common sense and make yourself accessible. Since access is what you want from them, it's only fair that *you're* easily accessible.

Subscribe to voice mail or get an answering machine. Get an E-mail address through an Internet provider or on-line service such as America Online or Prodigy; this costs less than $10 a month. Get a fax machine, or make arrangements with a nearby Kinko's or other retailer to receive faxes for you. Get an 800 number.

If you're not easy to reach, it's your own fault.

In Summary:

- The more you can envision your prospect's world, the more accurately you can predict how they will act.

- Organization Profiles and other research on your prospect's organization often yield useful information about the prospect.

- To truly get a feel for what motivates your prospect, put yourself in their shoes and imagine their typical day.

- To keep—and update—important information about your prospects, fill out a Prospect Portrait for each prospect and Leverage Point.

- Since access is what you want, make it quick, easy, and free for others to access you.

Eighteen

Preparation Step #5: Crystallize the Net Benefits of Your Offer

Part of your job is to communicate to each prospect the key benefits your offer can deliver to their organization. Because your prospects are always crunched for time, you must communicate these benefits quickly and clearly, so they're easy to remember. Here's how.

On a sheet of paper, make a bulleted list of *all* the specific benefits your offer can give your prospect. Each of these items *must* be:

- Real and concrete

- Measurable

- Provable

- Honest and ethical

- Directly related to the needs, goals, and objectives of your prospect's organization

Each of these benefits should also, directly or indirectly, affect your prospect *and* each of their Leverage Points in a positive way. *The more people who have something to gain from your offer, the more leverage you will be able to create.* Remember, many (maybe most) people won't act unless they see something in it for them. Therefore, the more people who feel they can personally benefit from your offer, the better off you are.

Once your list is complete, clarify and simplify each item, boiling it down to its essence. Each benefit should be a sound bite of ten words or less.

Now take a hard look at each benefit, and circle the three biggest, most important ones. Then order them, with the most important one first, so that you have either three short statements or one longer one that includes all three benefits. *This will become a litany you must memorize and be able to recite at any time.* For example: "The Circle of Leverage System will help you get in the door of your desired prospects *faster, more effectively,* and *with less expense.*" Or: "The Circle of Leverage will get you in the door *faster, better,* and *cheaper.*"

Write yours out. Shorten and tighten it until it's clear, focused, and concise. Your benefits must be bite-size and easy to remember, or your prospect will tune you out.

Practice saying these benefits until they roll off your tongue naturally, with certainty and confidence, and without hesitation.

Now you can confidently communicate to anyone, anywhere, any time the benefits of your offer—in a way that's easy to digest and comprehend. Don't forget, these key net benefits of your offer are part of why your prospect will pay attention to you.

In Summary:

- You must communicate the benefits of your offer quickly and clearly, in a way that's easy for your prospect to remember.

- These benefits must be real and concrete; measurable; provable; honest and ethical; and directly related to the needs, goals, and objectives of your prospect's organization.

- You can best communicate these benefits by turning them into brief sound bites, then identifying the three biggest, most important ones.

- Create a clear, simple litany out of these three key sound bites, then practice delivering it until it becomes second nature.

Preparation Step #6:
Know Your Competitors' Net Benefits
and Your Key Points of Difference—
Then Establish Your Position

Your competitors—those worth their salt—have done exactly what you've done in Preparation Step #5: They've crystallized the net benefits of their own offers. *Assume* your competitors can communicate these benefits as crisply as you can, in clear sound bites, bullet by bullet.

You're going to be competing head-to-head against these people and/or organizations. Never ignore what they're doing and hope that your benefits will sound bigger or better than theirs. You need to find out *exactly* what your competition is doing and saying. Then you must clearly position your offer against all the competition, by making it clear exactly how it is different.

This process, called *positioning*, has three stages:

1. Compare the net benefits of your own offer against those of each of your competitors.

2. Identify the key points of difference between your offer and your competitors'.

3. Create a positioning statement that clearly, concisely, and memorably expresses these key points of difference.

Evaluating the Competition

If you don't know who your competitors are, find out! Study the marketplace. Look at the professional journals in your (and your prospects') fields. Talk to people who are using a service, product, or concept similar to your own. If you're job hunting, arrange informational interviews with people in the line of work you want, and/or with their superiors.

Once you know who your primary competitors are, fill out the Competition Profile on page 168. List your five main competitors by name, in order of greatest visibility, reputation, or market share. If you're job-hunting, write down specific credentials, experience, or job titles other candidates might have (MBAs, sales and marketing directors, small business owners, etc.).

Now study each of your major competitors. Order and review their promotional materials. Look at their ads in consumer publications and/or trade journals. Get and study their annual reports. Check out their Web sites. Talk to their customers. Analyze their products and services—and their packaging and positioning. If you're looking for a job, find out what credentials, experience, and personality traits your competitors typically have.

This research will reveal the key net benefits of each of your competitor's offers. List these benefits on your Competition Profile in descending order of importance.

Now it's time to face the music. Look at the key net benefits of your offer and compare them against those of your competition, one by one. How is your offer better or different? How is it easier, faster, cheaper, more reliable, longer lasting, more durable, more flexible, safer, bigger, smaller, friendlier, cleaner, more attractive, more acces-

Competition Profile

Competitor #1 (name) _____

Benefit #1 _____

Benefit #2 _____

Benefit #3 _____

Positioning statement/slogan _____

Competitor #2 (name) _____

Benefit #1 _____

Benefit #2 _____

Benefit #3 _____

Positioning statement/slogan _____

Competitor #3 (name) _____

Benefit #1 _____

Benefit #2 _____

Benefit #3 _____

Positioning statement/slogan _____

Competitor #4 (name) _____

Benefit #1 _____

Benefit #2 _____

Benefit #3 _____

Positioning statement/slogan _____

Competitor #5 (name) _____

Benefit #1 _____

Benefit #2 _____

Benefit #3 _____

Positioning statement/slogan _____

sible? Is it backed by better support, better service, a better warranty? Does it do something that none of your competitors' offers can do?

The answers to these questions will become your *key points of difference*—those specific areas in which your offer excels or is unique. *You will position your offer against your competition by focusing on these key points of difference.*

You must have *one to three* points of difference. If you have more, condense them to the three most significant ones. If you have one or two, that's fine. But if you have zero, your prospect has no reason to grant you access.

Simplify and clarify these points of difference. You want to create a tight, easy-to-understand sound bite for each point of difference ("24-hour on-site service at no charge"), or a single brief statement that sums them all up ("The longest warranty and a no-questions-asked return policy").

Write these points of difference on the Positioning Worksheet on page 170. Rank these in order, with the most impressive or valuable one first. Practice repeating this information until it flows naturally and confidently.

Why are these key points of difference so important? Because your prospects and Leverage Points shouldn't have to spend any time analyzing the differences for themselves. They're being verbally pummeled by God knows how many other people trying to get in their doors. They lose the ability to differentiate, and after a while everything starts to blur together and sound the same. *Your key points of difference cut through the fog and help your prospects picture quickly how your offer is superior or unique—and worthy of their attention.*

This makes it easier on your prospects. *Don't make them work to figure out how you're different from your competition. You* must do the work and present those differences crisply. They'll appreciate your homework and clarity, and they'll feel that you are easier to work with, because you are easier to understand.

Think about the last time you went comparison-shopping for a product—say, a VCR, camcorder, or CD player. You looked at five different models, and they all probably looked pretty much the same. Didn't you appreciate (or wish for) someone who was able to go the extra step and explain exactly what the key points of difference were among the various models? Of course you did, because it made (or would have made) your decision easier.

Positioning Worksheet

The key benefits of my offer are:

Benefit #1 _____

Benefit #2 _____

Benefit #3 _____

Therefore, my offer's key points of difference are:

#1 _____

#2 _____

#3 _____

My positioning statement is:

_____

_____

When you present your key points of difference in a way that's easy to understand and remember, you make it much easier for your prospects to act in your favor. When you don't, the process becomes more painful for them and they will move away from you—toward someone else they feel can communicate clearly and simply.

Your Positioning Statement

If your offer is a product, service, or concept, there's another piece to this step you must not ignore. (If you're looking for a job, you can skip this section.)

Part of positioning means answering the question, *How do you want your prospect to picture your offer in their minds?*

Your key points of difference help your prospects quickly differentiate you from your competition—but you also want them to be able to quickly get a mental picture of your offer, so they remember it.

The tool for creating this picture is called a *positioning statement*: a catchy phrase, slogan, motto, or jingle. It can be a sentence ("We're the businessperson's airline"), a short phrase ("The on-time dry-cleaners"), a series of very brief statements ("Top quality. Top service. Not top dollar."), or even a single word ("Innovation"). Your positioning statement provides your prospect with a clear and easy way to picture—and remember—you or your offer. (Xerox's is "The Document Company.") It should wrap your offer's key benefits and key points of difference into one nice, neat little package. All they have to do is tug on the bow, and they can instantly picture and understand what makes your offer superior or unique.

Your positioning statement must of course be in line with the needs, goals, and objectives of your prospect's organization. If it isn't, you're wasting their time—and yours.

A classic example of an effective positioning statement is the one Avis used some years ago. In those days, Hertz was number one, the king of rental car companies. Avis was a major player but not in second place (though in the top ten). Avis created an ad campaign around the statement, "We're #2. We try harder." Avis positioned itself as "the other company," the other industry leader, Hertz's main competitor, a force to be reckoned with. At the same time, the statement drew attention to the key points of difference Avis wanted to communicate: better service and better-run operations. The campaign was a huge success and a self-fulfilling prophecy: Avis became the second-largest rental car company in the United States.

So play hotshot advertising executive. Study your offer's benefits and your key points of difference. Then brainstorm some possible positioning statements of your own. Remember, your statement should be short, catchy, and memorable, and should set your offer apart from everything else available.

When you've perfected your positioning statement, write it on your Positioning Worksheet.

In Summary:

- If you don't know who your competition is, find out!

- Assume your competitors can communicate the benefits of their own offers as clearly and concisely as you can.

- In order to compete, you must position your offer against your competition.

- Compare the net benefits of your offer against those of each competitor.

- Identify one to three key points of difference between your offer and your competitors'. Your offer *must* have at least one such difference.

- Sculpt these points of difference into crisp, clear sound bites.

- Develop a *positioning statement*: a catchy phrase, slogan, motto, or jingle that wraps your offer's greatest benefits and key points of difference into one nice, neat little package. This statement helps your prospects picture and remember the uniqueness of your offer. Plus, they'll believe you are much easier to deal with.

Twenty

Preparation Step #7:
Reality Check: Why Do You
Deserve to Get In?

Congratulations! You've got an offer that can clearly benefit each of your prospects in some genuine way. You can recite your offer's greatest benefits and key points of difference without hesitation. You've got a powerful, focused positioning statement that helps set you apart from your competition.

Now you're ready to make your move, right?

Wrong! Now you have all the ammunition you need to hit your target—*if* it's not moving. The problem is, in real life the target is usually moving. In fact, it's often *moving away from you—fast!* The real test of whether you deserve to get in is your willingness to go after that target and bring it to a halt.

Imagine you're in one of the most difficult prospecting situations ever. Your prospect is in the final stages of considering offers from a number of your competitors. A year ago a task force was formed to analyze the company's internal requirements and oversee the selection process. Nine months ago the task force issued a formal request for proposals. Since then it has reviewed the proposals carefully, met with a variety of your competitors, and recommended three finalists to the vice president, who will make a final selection within the next few weeks.

And now, late in the process, you find out about this opportunity. The formal deadline for accepting proposals is long past; in fact, the entire process is now completely out of the task force's hands. Your prospect is on a carefully planned track, moving methodically and quickly toward a decision, via a process everyone in the organization is happy with.

How do you get in the door?

If your first impulse is to say, "Forget it, it's too late," you're wrong. It's *not* too late, because a final decision has not yet been made. As Yogi Berra said, "It's not over until it's over."

In fact, in one way the situation is ideal: *Much of your competition has already been eliminated.* Only three competitors remain in the game.

So you go through the steps of the Circle of Leverage System, one by one. You figure out exactly what kind of access you need—in this case, because it's so late in the game, a thirty-minute in-person appointment very soon with the vice president, because she's the one making the final decision. You do some research on her company and its direct competitors to identify her Leverage Points. You envision how she's likely to feel and react when you suddenly appear, out of the blue, and start applying leverage. You crystallize the net benefits of your offer, establish your key points of difference, and establish your position against the three finalists.

Now jump ahead a bit. You've already sent out your initial communication to the vice president and three Leverage Points. You've let your message percolate for one or two days, in order to activate everyone's Key Engagers, so she feels the pressure of leverage from three directions. You place a follow-up call to her assistant. The assistant doesn't exactly sound delighted to hear from you, but she puts you through immediately. Suddenly you've got the vice president on the line, and you can hear the irritation in her voice. It's now or never.

What do you do?

Do you push ahead, engage your prospect, and press for the access you've requested—secure in the knowledge that your offer is as worthy as the other three finalists *and has at least one point of difference*, and confident that gaining access is in the best interest of both the vice president and her company?

Or do you back down, turn tail, or lose your confidence?

Be honest here.

If you can in good conscience push politely but firmly for access in this difficult situation, then you deserve to get in.

If you can't, you *don't* deserve access—*yet*. Something needs fixing, refining, or shoring up.

That's the whole point of this step—to help you pinpoint whatever problems or weaknesses remain, so you address them *before* you bring any leverage to bear on your prospects.

Ask yourself these questions, and be honest in answering them:

- Do I have doubts about the quality, value, or superiority of my offer?

- Am I being less than 100 percent honest about the benefits of my offer? Are any of my claims false or inflated?

- Can my presentation be more focused and refined?

- Have I been careless in identifying any prospects and/or Leverage Points?

- Have I failed to do all the necessary research on my prospect's organization? On my prospect? On my competitors and the benefits of their own offers?

- Are my offer's key net benefits and key points of difference less than 100 percent clear, accurate, and honest?

- Am I less than satisfied with my key points of difference or my positioning statement?

If the answer to any of these questions is yes, go back and address the problem. This could make the difference between getting access and being frozen out.

In Summary:

- "It isn't over until it's over." You can use the C.O.L. to help you gain access at *any* point in your prospect's decision-making process, even toward the very end.

- You're not ready to make your move until you're willing and able to go after a moving target in a difficult prospecting situation.

- If you can in good conscience push politely but firmly for access in such a situation, then you deserve to get in.

- If you can't, then you need to address any weaknesses before you continue with the next step of the C.O.L.

Twenty-One

Preparation Step #8: Crystallize the Net Benefits of Granting You Access

At this point *you're* convinced of all the reasons why you deserve access. In addition, you know in your head, heart, and gut all the ways your offer can benefit your prospects' organizations.

However, most of your prospects are looking for something more. They want to know what *they* will get out of granting you access—them *personally*, not the organizations they work for. *The benefits of your offer and the benefits of granting you access are two very different things.*

Most people are selfish. They want to know first and foremost, "What's in it for me?" If that's the question your prospect is asking, that's the question you must be prepared to answer in order to be let in their door.

Furthermore, your prospect knows that no one will realize any benefits from your offer unless their organization accepts it—and, from their point of view, that's a big "if," no matter how wonderful your offer sounds. Therefore, if they are going to invest their time in meeting or talking with you, they need to feel that they will win *just by letting you in*—even if they don't end up saying yes to your offer.

On the surface, your prospect may decide to consider your offer because it will help their organization do something faster, cheaper, or more effectively. But what your prospect *really* wants out of the transaction is:

- More security/less fear or uncertainty

- More approval/less disapproval

- More pleasure/less anxiety or stress

- More attention

- More recognition or prestige

- More power or authority

- More confidence

- More knowledge or awareness

- More money

In other words, they want more pleasure and less pain; more rewards and fewer risks.

Therefore you must *always* be ready to explain to your prospect exactly what they *will get* out of granting you access, regardless of whether they say yes to your offer. These direct, personal benefits are:

They'll have more security. Your prospect will feel more secure in knowing they've considered all the important options—or, at least, *your* important option—whether they accept your offer or not. ("You'll be able to say that you've looked at all the major players"; "For your investment of twenty minutes of time, you'll have the peace of mind of knowing that you looked into all the vendors that could save your company hundreds of thousands of dollars.")

They'll be more knowledgeable. The more your prospect knows, the wiser their decisions will be. ("You'll be in the best position to make the right decision—and much better informed on the entire subject.")

They'll have more confidence. Your prospect will be reassured that they're making the right decision. ("You'll be able to stand firmly behind your decision, without any doubts or second thoughts.")

Though you must not say it directly, your prospect will receive another major benefit by granting you access: freedom from the pressure of their Leverage Points.

Each of these benefits reduces their potential for pain (stress, anxiety, uncertainty, fear, risk) or increases their potential for pleasure (approval, recognition, security, status, power, money).

Normally it's not necessary to mention any of these personal benefits in your initial communication, though some people who use the C.O.L. do hint at them briefly in a sentence or two.

The time to put these in play is when you find yourself on the phone with your prospect, trying to convince them to give you the access you need. (They are also appropriate to mention *briefly* to secretaries and assistants: "I'm sure your boss wants to be able to stand 100 percent behind her final decision, without any doubts that she might have overlooked something important.")

You must be ready to recite these benefits at a moment's notice, so practice them aloud until they flow smoothly.

In Summary:

- The benefits of your offer and the benefits of granting you access are two very different things.

- Your prospect wants to know what *they* will get out of letting you in—whether or not they accept your offer.

- What your prospect *really* wants is more pleasure and less pain; more rewards and fewer risks.

- You must *always* be ready to explain to your prospect that, by granting you access:
  1. They will feel more *secure* in knowing that they've considered all the important options.
  2. They will be much more *knowledgeable*, and able to make wiser decisions.

3. They will be *confident and reassured* they're making the right decision.

- The best time to focus on these benefits is when you're on the phone with your prospect (or their assistant), pushing for the access you need.

- Practice reciting these benefits until they sound fluent and natural.

Twenty-Two

Preparation Step #9:
Take Stock of Your Firepower

You don't enter a battle without knowing exactly what weapons and ammunition you have available. In the same way, before you contact any prospects or Leverage Points, you must be aware of exactly what firepower you have at hand.

So ask yourself the following questions—and write down your answers. You may discover some firepower you didn't even realize existed.

1. Do you have any connection to your prospect, their organization, or anyone else in it? (This includes *any* business or personal relationships, potential referrals, etc.) Ask your colleagues, friends, family members, people from your church or synagogue, people from your club, friends of friends, people you know in your prospect's industry or town—*anyone* who might provide you with information or a referral.

2. Do you or your organization have a track record (ideally in your prospect's industry)? Do you have any statistics, testimonials, endorsements, or success stories that your prospect would view as impressive?

3. Do you possess the exact credentials your prospect wants—or superior ones?

4. Is your prospect's organization currently in desperate need of your offer? (Probably not, but it's always nice to know if they're searching for the type of thing you offer.)

5. Is someone else in your company already doing business with your prospect, or someone else in their organization? Have you or someone else in your company done business with them in the past? Did you or someone in your company previously work for your prospect, or their organization? If your prospect works for a large organization, they may not be aware of all such connections to you or your company. (And if *you* work for a large organization, you may not be aware of these connections until you ask around.) Every such connection, however small, may provide a useful bridge or referral.

6. Are you or your company doing business with one or more of your prospect's direct competitors? Were you previously employed by one of your prospect's competitors? If you or your company has a connection with an organization your prospect fears or admires (e.g., if you're approaching someone at IBM and one of your customers is Compaq), this will help you build additional leverage.

7. In your prospect's opinion (or the opinion of some of their Leverage Points), do you represent a well-known and well-respected name in your industry?

8. Do you hold an impressive title or position of responsibility? If you've got an impressive-sounding title, use it! And if you run your own company—even if it's a one-person business—declare yourself the president or director. Prospects love it when they're dealing with the people in charge. They feel more secure, more powerful, more connected, more hooked into the right person. *People respond faster and more positively to powerful-sounding titles*, even though most will deny it. Simply observe how people respond when Dr. Wilson or Father Michael is on the phone.

Don't advertise your title blatantly in neon lights, of course. Start out with something like this: "Hello, this is _____. I run the _____ division at _____." Or, "I'm in charge of _____ for _____." Don't worry—your prospects and Leverage Points will get it. A moment later, when you're leaving your name and phone number, you can slip in your official title.

It should go without saying that you must *never* manufacture a title you don't hold or deserve. Nothing destroys leverage faster than dishonesty.

After you've *written down* your answers to these questions, review them. Rank them in order of importance, impressiveness, or potential effectiveness. Then build the most impressive elements of firepower you possess into your strategy for getting in the door, by using them in your initial communication to your prospect and Leverage Points. (We'll go through this in detail in Chapter 24.)

A Word of Caution About Referrals

Most people—even friends, family, and co-workers—want to be perceived as well-connected and in the know. This can get you into trouble when they offer you a referral—no matter how sincere and eager to help they might be.

Many years ago, when a company I had started needed a short-term loan, I bumped into someone I knew slightly on a professional basis. I mentioned I was bank shopping. Without hesitation, he threw out the name of a bank president. "Call him; use my name. He's been a big help in the past. Here's his number." So I called the bank president, who promptly asked who had referred me to him. I mentioned the man's name. The president was surprised. "*He* gave you my name?" "Yes," I said, "he said he knows you well." "Sure I do. What was it you wanted, anyway?" As it turned out, the president had no respect at all for the man, who had gone bankrupt. As a result of his referral, my credibility with this bank president instantly went *down* ten notches—before the president even knew what I was calling about.

Another example: I was at the club where I work out, watching a middle-aged man talking with a very attractive woman on the Nordic Track. It was clear from their conversation that they didn't know each other very well. She was explaining that she was trying to get in to see somebody, and wasn't having any success. He was doing his best to impress her with his connectedness: "Honey, you call _____ and

183

tell him I told you to call. Use my name. If you have any trouble, you call me and I'll call him for you." Judging by how hard he was pushing the point, it looked to me that his primary motivation wasn't to help her get access, but to sell himself to her.

The point here is that a referral from the wrong person can destroy some or all of your leverage. Some referrals are sugar-coated time bombs waiting to go off. *Never* assume that all referrals are good referrals, or that anyone's connections are as close as they claim. Instead, *always* check out and verify each referral you are given, *before* you use it. If you don't, you could blow your entire attempt to get in.

How do you check out a referral? Simple: Ask the referrer for details. Here are some questions you might ask:

- How are you connected with this person?

- How have you dealt with them? In what context?

- How well do you know this person?

- How long have you known them?

- How close are you?

- When were you last in contact?

- Will they recognize your name?

- How do they view you?

- What is the history of your relationship?

No one making a *legitimate* referral will be offended by any of these questions, because they'll recognize you're just doing your homework. If someone does get upset, or gives vague or elusive answers, it's usually a strong sign that something's not quite right and that their referral is highly suspect.

Back when I wanted that loan, I blew a perfectly good opportunity to build a relationship with a bank, all because I didn't do the basic homework of asking my referrer three minutes' worth of simple questions. Don't let yourself be set back by the same oversight.

In Summary:

- Before you contact any prospects or Leverage Points, be aware of exactly what firepower you have at hand. Ask yourself these questions:

  * Do you have any connection to your prospect, their organization, or anyone else in it?

  * Do you or your organization have a track record?

  * Do you possess the exact credentials your prospect wants?

  * Is your prospect's organization in desperate need of your offer?

  * Is someone else in your company already doing business with your prospect or with someone else in the organization? Have you or someone else in your company done business with them in the past?

  * Are you or your company doing business with one or more of your prospect's direct competitors?

  * Do you represent a well-known and well-respected name in your industry?

  * Do you hold an impressive title or position of responsibility?

- Rank your answers in order of importance, impressiveness to your prospect, or potential effectiveness. Then build them into your strategy for getting in the door—the most impressive ones first.

- A referral from the wrong person can destroy some or all your leverage—so never assume that all referrals are good referrals, or that people's connections are as close as they claim.

- Whenever you are given a referral, check out its validity by asking the referrer for significant details.

Twenty-Three

Preparation Step #10:
Check Your Attitude

You're almost ready to draw a circle of leverage around each of your prospects. All you need to do is make sure you're in the right frame of mind.

Demonstrate That You're Prepared

Recite aloud the three biggest benefits of your offer, with the greatest one first. Be ready to focus on this single most profound benefit when necessary.

State your key points of difference among your competitors.

Repeat your positioning statement.

Refine and rehearse the presentation you plan to make until it is sharp, properly structured, precise, and memorable.

Remind Yourself That You *Deserve* to Get In

Why? Because you have an offer that will truly benefit your prospects' organizations, and because getting the access you need is a genuine win-win opportunity for you *and* your prospects.

Visualize yourself in your prospect's office, making your presentation. Imagine that several people are watching and listening, absorbed in your words. Expect that this will soon be a reality.

Allow Yourself to Make Mistakes

I have blown plenty of good opportunities to get in over the past fifteen years. I've been unfocused, not crisp or clear, too soft, angry, lazy and unprepared, too casual—you name it. But that's how I learned the art of gaining access.

You'll mess up sometimes, too. How can you expect not to? But in the process, you'll get better and better at using the Circle of Leverage System.

In the game of getting in, as in most things, everybody knows that the people who screw up the most, learn from their mistakes, and keep trying are the ones who become the masters of the game.

Review Your Mind-Set

Check for and reflect on these attitudes, one by one:

- A quiet confidence in yourself, your offer, and the research you've done

- A commitment to your offer, based on its real value to your prospects' organizations

- An awareness that you're far better prepared than most or all of your competition

- A clear sense that getting in is often a self-fulfilling prophecy—which is why you must *expect* to get in

- A readiness to move forward

Take the Pest Test

Now give yourself one final test. Ask yourself this question: *Do I feel that I'm bothering my prospects in any way by trying to get in their doors?*

If you answered with a firm no, you've passed the pest test with flying colors. You're ready to make your move.

In Summary:

As the final pieces of preparation before beginning your Execution Steps:

1. Demonstrate that you're prepared.

2. Remind yourself that you deserve to get in.

3. Accept that you'll make mistakes, especially at first.

4. Review your mind-set.

5. Take the pest test.

Making Your Move: The Five Execution Steps of the Circle of Leverage System

Twenty-Four

Execution Step #1:
Prepare Your Initial Communication
and Put It in Play

About the Five Execution Steps

The Execution Steps presented in this section require timing, delicacy, precision, confidence, and *practice*. Because getting in your prospect's door is different every time, there's not always an obvious, set pattern to follow. With experience you will get better at making seat-of-the-pants judgments and decisions.

While each of the five Execution Steps is a separate process, when you're in the heat of execution some or all of them will run together very quickly. That's normal, so expect it. They're broken down into steps the way they are so you can understand the necessity of each one.

Making Contact

Begin drawing a circle of leverage around each of your prospects by sending out a simple but carefully written letter of one to two pages.* Each prospect and Leverage Point gets their own personally addressed copy; time all copies to arrive on the same day. If you're approaching more than one organization in the same industry or area, you can create maximum leverage by having every prospect and Leverage Point in every organization receive your letter at once.

You may send these letters by regular mail, fax, courier, or Express Mail. E-mail is *not* an option for using the C.O.L., except in special cases (e.g., your prospects and Leverage Points work in the computer industry). It's too easy for your message to get lost in the river of E-mails most computer users receive, and it's too easy for people to simply ignore or delete it.

The transport vehicle you select for your letter will be based on urgency, cost, and need for visibility. Here are the pros and cons of each vehicle:

Regular mail. Pros: reliable and inexpensive. Cons: can be slow to Alaska, Hawaii, and distant rural areas. You may need to mail letters on different days to ensure they arrive at all your recipients' offices on the same day.

Fax. Pros: inexpensive, highly visible, and immediate; provides acknowledgment that your message was received. Con: if two or more of your recipients share the same fax machine, a secretary may collect the faxes, see that they are virtually identical, and reduce or shut down your leverage by throwing some of them away or delivering them all to the same person. Many small companies have one central fax, which is shared by all employees. (I usually don't send C.O.L. letters by fax if two or more of my targeted recipients share the same fax number. It's much too easy to be blocked by assistants.)

Courier and Express Mail. Pros: quick, highly visible, slightly impressive. Con: can be expensive.

---

*If time is extremely tight (e.g., you've just learned of an opportunity where your prospect is very close to making a final decision) *and* you have excellent telephone skills, you may wish to deliver your initial message by phone. For complete details on this option and a sample C.O.L. phone message, see pages 260–262. *I do not recommend this option until you have become proficient at using the C.O.L.*

Normally I send my C.O.L. letters by first class mail, though I have used every one of the above options.

Look at Chapters 9 and 24 for detailed guidance on how to write an effective C.O.L. letter. You'll also find, on pages 98–99, an actual C.O.L. letter that I used (with some minor modifications) to gain access to a number of very large law firms. Sample layouts for two additional Circle of Leverage letters follow, on pages 194–197. Feel free to use any of these as a model.

The Essential Eleven

From your recipient's point of view, your letter must quickly and clearly answer eleven essential questions that arise in their mind. You must design your message so that it answers all of these questions, more or less in the order given below. This is the order in which these questions normally arise in your recipient's mind. The answers to these questions help them come to a quick decision regarding your request for access.

The Essential Eleven are:

1. Who are you?

2. What do you do? (What is your title or level of responsibility? At what firm?)

3. Why are you sending this to me? (What's your connection to me? How did you get my name?)

4. Who else are you sending this message to?

5. What's this about?

6. What do you want from me?

7. When do you want it?

8. How long will it take?

9. Who needs to be involved? (optional)

10. How will it benefit my organization? (Why should I care?)

11. Who else do you do this for? (Who else are you contacting or dealing with in my industry?) (optional)

Date

Name of recipient
Title of recipient
Company name
Address

Dear (first name only):

#1 WHO ARE YOU?
#2 WHAT DO YOU DO?

#4 WHO ELSE ARE YOU
SENDING THIS MESSAGE TO?
(Begin to create
leverage right away.)
#3 WHY ARE YOU SENDING
THIS TO ME?

As [your title] of [name of your organization], I am writing to you, [first and last name of Leverage Point #1], [first and last name of Leverage Point #2], and [first and last name of Leverage Point #3] to determine who is the most appropriate person in your company to meet with for ___ minutes during the week of _____.

#5 WHAT'S THIS ABOUT?
#10 HOW WILL IT BENEFIT
MY ORGANIZATION?

[Name of your organization] offers [very brief description of your offer], which can [three biggest benefits, each in ten words or less, with the greatest benefit first].

After doing some research on [name of recipient's organization], I've learned that you have _____, _____, and _____ [specific needs], and I think we might be able to help.

#11 WHO ELSE DO YOU DO THIS FOR?	We currently do business with _____, _____, and _____ [names of organizations that compete with recipient's employer and/or your other well-known customers]. Using our product/service, they have
(Drive home your benefits again.)	_____, _____, and _____ [specific results obtained].
#6 WHAT DO YOU WANT FROM ME?	If this is of interest, I would like to schedule a twenty-minute appointment during [time period] to
#7 WHEN DO YOU WANT IT?	learn about your specific needs in this area to see if we can help. To provide the best use of everyone's
#8 HOW LONG WILL IT TAKE?	time, I recommend that the following people be involved: _____, _____, and _____.
#9 WHO NEEDS TO BE INVOLVED?	I will follow up shortly with your executive assistant to find out if you've seen this letter and if you wish to schedule the appointment. Please let them know your answer so I may schedule it through them.

Thank you for your time.

Sincerely,

Sample Circle of Leverage Letter #2

Date

Name of recipient
Title of recipient
Company name
Address

Dear (first name only):

#4 WHO ELSE ARE YOU
SENDING THIS MESSAGE TO?
#3 WHY ARE YOU SENDING
THIS TO ME?
#6 WHAT DO YOU WANT
FROM ME?
#7 WHEN DO YOU WANT IT?
#8 HOW LONG WILL IT
TAKE?
#11 WHO ELSE DO YOU DO
THIS FOR?

I'm writing to you, [first and last name of Leverage Point #1], [first and last name of Leverage Point #2], and [first and last name of Leverage Point #3], to find the most appropriate person or people to deal with regarding scheduling a twenty-minute in-person appointment on March 10th or 11th, when I plan to be in town meeting with the directors of purchasing of several of the area's largest firms in the industry.

#1 WHO ARE YOU?
#2 WHAT DO YOU DO?
#5 WHAT'S THIS ABOUT?

#10 HOW WILL IT BENEFIT
MY ORGANIZATION?

At [name of your organization], where I am [your title], our business is helping companies such as yours to [very brief description of your offer]. The net benefits we deliver are [three biggest benefits, with the greatest benefit first]. Our key point of difference is _____, and we are proud of our position as the _____ of _____.

#6 WHAT DO YOU WANT FROM ME?

#8 HOW LONG WILL IT TAKE?
#7 WHEN DO YOU WANT IT?
#6 WHAT DO YOU WANT FROM ME?

#9 WHO NEEDS TO BE INVOLVED?

If you grant the appointment, what I will present is [brief description of key points of your presentation, focused on benefits]. When I follow up with your assistant in the next couple of days, please let them know if you wish to schedule the twenty-minute appointment and what times are good for you. Otherwise, please direct me to the appropriate person you want me to deal with regarding getting together.

Thank you. I look forward to meeting you.

Sincerely,

If you have any additional information that may impress your recipient or activate their Key Engagers—e.g., you were referred to them by a customer or mutual acquaintance, or you used to work for their organization, or your offer has recently received media attention—include this *very briefly* as well.

If you are targeting competing companies in your recipient's industry, use that information as additional leverage—e.g., "In early June I expect to meet with the general managers of the seven largest automobile dealerships in your area." (Saying "expect to" or "plan to" enables you to make this statement honestly even though you have not yet booked a single meeting or conference. The statement must be true, however—that is, you must indeed be planning what you say you're planning.)

Your letter should close with the information that you will be following up by phone shortly to find out their response. This lets your recipient know that they will not have the opportunity to ignore you.

Other Points to Remember

- Refer to each recipient by their first name ("Dear Marilyn") unless you have good reason to do otherwise.

- All your initial messages *must* arrive as close to simultaneously as possible.

- Each letter should be personally addressed to the recipient and sent separately. *Never* send two or more letters in the same envelope or fax.

- All your prospects and Leverage Points must receive essentially the same letter. The only things that should change are names, addresses, lists of Leverage Points, and items that pertain to particular recipients (e.g., a referral).

Once your C.O.L. letter has been delivered, the game begins. If you follow the next execution step properly, and are careful in what you do, you may win that game in the first or second round.

In Summary:

- During the heat of execution, some or all of the Execution Steps will run together.

- Make initial contact with your prospects and Leverage Points via a one- or two-page C.O.L. letter. You may send this letter by regular mail, fax, courier, or Express Mail.

- Each recipient gets a personally addressed, separately delivered letter.

- Each letter must answer the Essential Eleven questions on page 193, more or less in order.

- All of your letters should arrive as close to simultaneously as possible.

Twenty-Five

Execution Step #2:
Flush Out Your Prospect

Making a 180-Degree Turn

This is the most important chapter in the whole book—so I'm going to begin by framing this second Execution Step so you can most easily picture it.

Let's review what you've done to get to this point.

Step One: You've defined what you need versus what you want, so granting your request for access should be easy and painless for your prospects.

Step Two: You've done your homework, so you're knowledgeable about your prospects, their Leverage Points, and their organizations.

Step Three: You've chosen your prospects, as well as two or more Leverage Points for each prospect. These key people will trigger four very simple yet powerful emotions in your prospects, causing them to want to pay attention to you.

Step Four: You've used your background research to fill out Prospect Portraits for all of your prospects, so you understand their nature and can empathize with them. This will help you predict how they will respond.

Step Five: You've concisely defined the three key net benefits of your offer.

Step Six: You've studied and know the key net benefits of your competition and can clearly communicate your key points of difference in relation to your competitors. In addition, you've decided on a positioning statement that crisply communicates your offer, thus making it easier for your prospects to understand and remember.

Step Seven: You've analyzed your offer and presentation, have addressed any weaknesses, and are confident that you deserve to get in because of the value your offer will provide.

Step Eight: You've crystallized the net benefits of granting you access, so your prospects know how they'll benefit even if they don't accept your offer.

Step Nine: You've analyzed your firepower and selected your most potent weapons.

Step Ten: You've taken the pest test and know your attitude is in the right place.

Next you've taken all the appropriate information and placed it inside the C.O.L. letter you drafted. You put the letter in play by sending it to your prospects and Leverage Points.

Now . . . let me remind you that you are more prepared, more focused, more knowledgeable, and more likely to be granted access than 95 percent of your competitors. And you have communicated your message and request for access more clearly and crisply than your competition. (This alone makes you stand out above the clutter.) Now that your communication is about to land in your prospects' and Leverage Points' hands, you're about to realize the full power of the System.

At this point, what you've been taught about how to prospect, what you've been taught is proper and appropriate, and what your common sense would suggest, is to follow up your letter with a phone call, blow past the secretaries, get your prospects and Leverage Points on the phone, and convince them to grant your request for access by pitching the benefits of your offer. I mean, it's common sense, right?

Wrong! This is *not* what you want to do next, unless you wish to totally destroy the leverage that you're about to activate.

Remember what you're doing here: You're using a process that activates in your prospects and Leverage Points four very powerful emotions—emotions that are a heck of a lot more important and meaningful to them than the net benefits of your offer. So if you go blasting past the secretaries and machine-gun your prospects—who are tired, stressed out, busy, and for the most part uninterested—with the benefits of your wonderful offer, you should hit yourself in the head with a bat. If you start blasting away, you will destroy all your efforts.

This is the fundamental difference between what has been (and still is) taught about prospecting and how the C.O.L. works.

You do *not* want to get your prospects or Leverage Points on the phone. Nor is this the time for your sales pitch on the wonderful benefits of your offer. It's simply time to follow up with the assistants of every recipient of your letter to find out the answers to these simple questions:

1. Did the prospect or Leverage Point see your communication and read it? *Yes or no.*

2. Do they wish to grant your request for access? *Yes or no.* (If yes, then schedule the meeting or conference immediately.)

3. Did they or their assistant route your letter to someone else? If so, find out:

    • The name and title of that person

    • Their relationship to the original recipient of your letter

    • If the new recipient is aware that the letter is coming

    • When they should receive it

    • If a message was sent along with it (e.g., "This looks interesting. Check it out and report back.")

- Who did the routing—the original recipient or their assistant?

That's it—that's *all* you want to know. And while you're following up and collecting those responses, in the background the four Key Engagers are quietly working their magic on each of your recipients. This is what helps you flush out your prospect and get you in their door.

For those of you saying, "You're crazy. This is weird," remember what I said earlier. *You've got to trust the power of the C.O.L.* It works if you use it correctly, and if you *allow* it to work. Its power is based on a simple, basic psychological process.

Flushing out your prospect means doing the following:

1. Allow one to two business days after your communication has been received for it to percolate in the hearts, minds, and emotions of each recipient.

2. Follow up by phone with the assistant of every one of your prospects and Leverage Points—always going in order from the highest to the lowest-ranking person—with the goal of getting the answers to the above questions.

Again, the goal is to get these nuggets of information from assistants, not the actual people you've targeted. Why? Because if you do get a prospect or Leverage Point on the phone, they can force bits and pieces of your presentation out of you, even though they're not really in the right frame of mind to receive it. As a result, you will lose leverage and can get shot down more easily. Besides, you've already made a condensed version of your presentation in your letter. Everything they need to know to grant your request is in there.

Because you never know who your ultimate prospect will end up being, you must diligently keep following up with everyone who received your letter, going from the highest rank to the lowest, while the System activates the Key Engagers of each recipient.

As you collect responses, a picture begins to be painted, with arrows pointing to your ultimate prospect. This is the person you want to call last—once you are armed with the most knowledge and your most powerful leverage.

This process amazes me every time I use it, because it's so powerful and simple.

Switching Paradigms

When I reach this Execution Step in my C.O.L. training workshops, it takes a while for what I've said to sink in. I'm asking people to make a fundamental change in their thinking, and that's not easy. I've learned that for people to truly understand this step, and to make a real mental shift, they need me to explain this step a second time, in a slightly different way. So now I'm going to lay it out again—in more detail, and from a different angle.

To carry out this second Execution Step—and for the C.O.L. to work properly—you must do *exactly the opposite* of what you're used to doing.

If you've had any traditional training in sales or marketing, you know that every prospector has four goals for their first phone call to a new prospect: (1) get past the secretary or assistant; (2) talk directly to the prospect; (3) give the prospect a quick spiel about the benefits of your offer; and (4) use these benefits as the sole justification for why they should grant you a meeting or conference.

With the Circle of Leverage System, you do *none* of these.

You don't try to get past secretaries and assistants. Instead, you work *with* them.

You don't try to talk directly to your prospects. In fact, until you're actually in a meeting or conference with your prospect, your goal is to *avoid* talking to them. You avoid talking directly to Leverage Points as well. Why? Because they'll often force you into a "quick pitch" over the phone when *they're* not really in the right state of mind to receive it. Plus, in your letter you've already presented your offer's benefits and made your request for access as concisely as you can.

If you do end up having to talk with your prospect or Leverage Point on the phone, *you must avoid being dragged into giving your presentation*.

And *you **never** rely on the benefits of your offer to provide the necessary horsepower to get the access you need*. Again, you let the C.O.L. do its work behind the scenes.

If you're feeling confused right now, that's normal. You're probably thinking, "Wait a minute. I've been taught over and over that if I can get my prospect on the phone, that's my big chance. Now you're

204

telling me to not even try. It sounds crazy!" That's a very natural response, too.

Remember how I told you in the early chapters of this book that the C.O.L. is a totally new, different, and vastly more effective way to gain access to your prospects?

If you're like most people, when you read those words, you thought, "Oh, I see. This is a new way I can get prospects to talk with me on the phone, so I can tell them about my offer and coax them into letting me in their doors."

Wrong, wrong, wrong.

Most of the time, *the C.O.L. enables you to skip the entire process of talking your way in.* Instead, it quickly delivers either the access you desire—*without any discussion or interim steps*—or a firm, unequivocal no. There's no wondering, very little waiting, and a minimum of prevaricating on your prospect's part.

You must trust the C.O.L. to do its job. Meanwhile, *your* job is to *stay out of the way* as people talk behind the scenes, worry about what to do, discuss your request, sometimes disagree, and pass your letter from person to person.

All you need to do is make some brief follow-up calls, ask a few key questions, write down the answers, and continue following up by phone until your *real* prospect bubbles to the surface and responds to your request for access.

Many people find it hard to believe that the C.O.L. works like it does. It just seems too easy. But if you are to successfully carry out this single most important step, you must leave all of your old lessons, attitudes, and notions behind. If you follow the guidance in this and other chapters, the C.O.L. *will* work for you—not all the time, of course, but often enough to make it extremely valuable. *You must trust the System and allow it to work its magic.*

Nevertheless, the care, focus, and exactness with which you perform this step can mean the difference between getting in and getting shut out. You must have your wits about you, because this step often involves precision moves. Sloughing off, laziness, or unfocused energy can all undermine your leverage.

As I've said, you can never know in advance exactly who your ultimate prospect—the real decision maker(s)—will be in any organization. Sometimes it will be one of your original Leverage Points. Sometimes it will be someone you hadn't written to or even known about. Therefore, *you must systematically flush out your real prospect* by following up your letter with a series of phone calls to the assistants of the people you've targeted.

You want the answers to the following simple questions:

1. **Did your intended recipient get and review your communication?** *Yes or no*.

2. **Do they wish to grant the access you requested?** *Yes or no*.

3. **Did they (or their assistant) route your communication to someone else to handle? To whom?**

Let me repeat: **You do not want to get your prospects and Leverage Points on the phone.** This is *not* the time for a sales pitch on the wonderful benefits of your offer. And you *don't* want to schmooze your way past anyone. *All you want are the answers to these simple questions!* Your goal is just to get these nuggets of information, preferably from your prospects' and Leverage Points' assistants.

Letting the Power of Percolation Work

Wait one to two business days after your letters arrive before making your follow-up calls. This gives your letters the right amount of time to percolate in the hearts and minds of your prospects and Leverage Points. Their Key Engagers are activated, causing them to interact with each other in regard to your request for access. There may be behind-the-scene discussions, meetings, disagreements, even power struggles over who should handle your request and how they should handle it. All of this interaction makes your leverage stronger—and helps you flush out who your real prospect is.

Before you begin your follow-up calls, I suggest you spread out in front of you your filled-in Circle of Leverage forms (from page 90 or 156, one for each prospect), your partially filled-in Prospect Portraits (from page 160, one for each prospect), and your Organization Profiles (from pages 73–75, one for each organization). As you make your follow-up calls, add any useful information to these forms in the appropriate spots.

The most important forms to update are the C.O.L. forms. Indicate on these when you made each call, whose assistant or voice mail you spoke to, and what response (if any) you received. Also add information on any new potential prospects as you receive responses.

Your first round of calls should be made all at once. *Always begin with the highest-ranking person in your prospect's organization who received your letter, then systematically work your way down* until you've called every recipient. However, save your prospect for last, regardless of where they appear in the hierarchy. If, in the flushing-out process, someone you didn't expect emerges as your ultimate prospect, rearrange your order of calls so that you follow up with them last of all.

Remember, you don't want to speak directly with prospects and Leverage Points. Your goal is to get responses from their assistants. If this is not possible—if the assistant is on vacation all week, or the person has no assistant—then select the best option you can from the list below (in descending order of desirability):

- Your prospect or Leverage Point's voice mail. With this option you get to control exactly what the person hears.

- Their assistant's voice mail.

- The secretary or receptionist for the department, floor, or whole organization.

- A substitute, temporary, or floating assistant.

- The prospect or Leverage Point themselves. This is not a desirable option, because they can all too easily force you into giving some of your presentation on the phone. You want to avoid this. Besides, you've already explained your offer in your letter.

- Voice mail for the entire organization, division, unit, department, or office.

Make each of your calls through the organization's main switchboard or receptionist. Begin by asking, "Does _____ have an assistant, or voice mail, or both?" If they have an assistant, get that person's name and phone number. Write the answers on your C.O.L.

form for easy reference. Then ask to be transferred to the appropriate extension.

Each follow-up call should follow roughly the same pattern, regardless of whether you reach your prospect or Leverage Point, their assistant, someone else, or voice mail. (Your C.O.L. voice mail messages will have to be fairly lengthy in order to cover everything described below, but that's fine.)

Making the Call

This section leads you through a typical conversation with a secretary. However, it also applies—with common sense modifications—to talking with prospects, Leverage Points, and people's voice mail.

Begin by making sure you're speaking with the person most directly connected to your prospect or Leverage Point. "Hi. Is this [assistant's first name], [boss's name]'s assistant?" If it's not, ask to be transferred to them.

Then explain, *without pausing*:

- Who you are (including, if appropriate, your title and/or level of responsibility).

- Why you're calling—i.e., to learn whether your recipient has received and reviewed your message, and to find out if they wish to grant your request for access.

- Who else has received your initial message. This is essential, because it immediately reminds the person of the leverage you have created.

For example: "Kim, this is Michael Boylan, President of The Boylan Group in Minneapolis. I'm calling about a letter I sent to Justin dated April second, in which I requested a meeting with him later in the month. I also sent similar faxes to _____, _____, and _____ [Justin's internal Leverage Points]."

Again *without pausing*, ask the secretary if they have time to take your name and phone number. If they say yes, give that information. (If they *don't* have time, ask when would be a good time to call back, and do so then.)

208

Then, *once more without pausing*, make it clear that you don't need to speak directly to their boss. For example: "Kim, I really don't need to speak to your boss at all if you can answer a few quick questions for me. In fact, I'd prefer to take direction from you on this, if that's all right." (Of course it's all right with them. They love this statement because it makes them feel as if they are in control of the whole process.)

Next, ask if their boss has received your message. Presumably they have. If they haven't, fax a new one ASAP and follow up again in another one to two days.

Ask if their boss has *read* your message yet, and if they wish to grant your request. If the answer is yes, schedule it. If it's no, ask if they know why. Once they've answered that question—even if their answer is "I don't know" or "He didn't say"—thank them and end the call.

If the assistant doesn't have a yes or no for you yet, ask where the letter is now—on their boss's desk, routed to someone else, etc.

If their boss hasn't routed your letter, then make this straightforward request: "Will you see or speak to him today or tomorrow? Could you see whether he's interested in granting my request for an appointment? If I haven't heard from you by _____, I'll call back to find out his response. Does that work for you?"

Last, remind the assistant of the leverage you've created by saying that you'll be following up all your letters: "Thank you. As you know, Kim, letters also went out to _____, _____, and _____, and since I promised each of them I would follow up by phone, I'll be doing that shortly to find out their responses as well. Thanks again for your time. Good-bye."

This sounds almost too simple, I know. But unless the letter has been routed to someone else, *it's all you need to do for now*. In fact, if you do any more, you'll only get in your own way. As you collect these responses, a picture will begin to be painted of who your real prospect is. The C.O.L. will take care of the rest.

If you haven't gotten a response to your first call to someone, follow up again in two to four business days (or at some other agreed-upon time). Be 100 percent straightforward and direct—no schmoozing or sales pitches. Make it clear that all you want is an answer to your request for access. For example: "Hi, Kim, this is Michael Boylan. We spoke on Monday regarding my letter to Justin dated April second that also went to _____, _____, and _____. Do you know of his response?"

If the assistant still doesn't have an answer, explain politely that you will continue to follow up by phone until you get a definite response. Keep calling until you have a clear yes, no, or referral to someone else in the organization.

Now let's follow a scenario in which your letter has been routed to someone else. In this situation, you need to ask the assistant several more questions:

- Did your boss route it, or was it routed before they had a chance to see or read it? This makes a difference! If the boss did the routing, that gives you much more leverage with whomever receives it.

- Who was the letter routed to? Get this person's name, title, and phone number, as well as the name and phone number of their assistant. This person will become your new, tentative prospect. Add them to your list of calls to make and to your C.O.L. form.

- What is this other person's relationship to your boss? Are they the boss's superior, their direct report, etc.?

- On what date was the letter forwarded?

- On what date is the person likely to receive it?

- Are they aware the letter is on its way?

- Did your boss send a message of their own with the letter? What did the message say? For example, "Check this out and report back to me, would you?"

Get whatever answers the assistant can give you, thank them, and hang up.

Once the letter has percolated in the mind of this new recipient for one to two business days, give their assistant a call and repeat the process:

- Did they see it?

- Do they wish to grant an appointment?

- Did the letter get routed to someone else? Who did the routing?

Once you have gotten detailed answers to your questions, you will be informed, confident, and on top of the situation.

The Final Word

Eventually, each prospect and Leverage Point is going to do one of six things. Here's how to respond to each one:

1. They grant your request for access. *Immediately* book the appointment or conference. Don't talk about the benefits of your offer or go overboard in expressing your gratitude or delight. Nail down a day and time, and get off the phone.

Immediately stop making follow-up calls to anyone else in the organization. Don't take the chance of shooting yourself in the foot and undoing what you've already accomplished by stirring things up further. You've been granted the access you need, so your work is done. The C.O.L. delivered.

You can assume that the people who received your letter (and/ or their assistants) will spread the word that the situation has been handled and a meeting or conference has been scheduled.

2. They give you a clear no. While the C.O.L. has an excellent track record of getting people in the door, it does not work 100 percent of the time. It will get your message in front of people and get them to take it seriously. But if someone refuses you access, graciously thank them for the response, hang up, and make no more calls to them.

However, *continue to follow up with every other person your letter went to in the organization.* **It's quite common for one person to say no, only to have someone else in the organization grant you access by overruling or disagreeing with the person who said no.**

3. They route your letter to someone else. See the previous section of this chapter.

4. They ask you to send more information on your offer. Do this, but send a very limited amount, packaged in bite-size chunks. (Remember, this should be carefully designed to intrigue them and whet their appetite for more. It should *not* give them enough information to make a decision on your offer.)

A few days later, call their assistant or voice mail again and ask whether or not they wish to grant your request for access. Once again, avoid pitching the benefits of your offer. You can do that once you're in!

5. <u>**They ask you to tell them more about your offer on the phone.**</u> Briefly explain your offer's key net benefits and your positioning statement. Recite the names of some of your other major customers (if appropriate). Add a few other bits of pertinent information. Then explain that the best way to understand your offer is through an in-person appointment (or whatever form of access you've requested). Repeat your request for access. As necessary, dance, sponge, and reiterate (see Chapter 26 for details).

Whenever you're asked for "more information" in unspecified form, agree to send something by mail.

I repeat: *Always try to avoid getting drawn into your presentation over the phone.* This makes it easy for your prospect to say no to your offer before you've gotten the access you need.

6. <u>**They fail to respond to your letter or follow-up calls.**</u> If someone doesn't respond to three follow-up calls in a row, write them off. A fourth call isn't going to help, and will probably be perceived as annoying. Focus your attention on other people in that organization.

Some Common "What Ifs"

<u>What if you learn in a follow-up call to someone powerful that they have routed your letter to someone lower down?</u> Call the person to whom it was routed, of course—but not until you naturally reach them in your process of calling the most powerful people first and working your way down through the hierarchy. This is important, because it's possible that someone higher up in the organization might grant you access first—and the higher the level at which you get in, the better.

<u>What if an assistant tells you that their boss has received your</u>

letter but not yet read it? Urge them to ask their boss for a response. Mention the other people in the organization who have also received copies and explain that you are in the process of following up with them as well. Add that you'll call back in another few days to get their boss's response to your request, and do so.

What if a secretary wants to connect you to their boss? Say something like this: "I really don't need to talk with them. In fact, I'd prefer to take direction from you on this." If the secretary *still* wants you to speak with their boss ("She books all her own appointments, so you really need to talk to her"), of course agree. Then dance, sponge, and reiterate (see Chapter 26) as necessary until you get your response— yes or no.

What if two different people in the same organization each want to schedule an appointment or conference? Inform them of each other's interest, and schedule a single appointment (ideally with both in attendance).

What if a prospect or Leverage Point returns your call by leaving a message on your voice mail asking what your call was about? Follow up with their assistant or voice mail in exactly the same way you would if they hadn't returned your call. This puts the focus right back on the leverage you've created.

What if someone calls to grant you access before you can even make a follow-up call to their office? Congratulations! You've used the C.O.L. effectively. Book the appointment or conference at once. (This does happen, by the way.)

What if, before you have a chance to make any follow-up calls, one of your recipients responds by turning down your request for access? Make your follow-up calls to everyone else in the organization anyway. *The person who turned you down may not be your ultimate prospect.* In fact, if the person who delivered the message is a secretary, they may be acting entirely on their own, and their boss may not have even gotten or read your letter. Remember, everyone has their own agenda. I've been in hundreds of situations where lower-level people have responded, "No, thank you, we're not interested," only to get calls later from more senior-level people I've targeted, saying, "Great, come on in."

Tips to Remember When Flushing Out
Your Prospect

1. Never forget that you are playing a game—a game of power, timing, perceptions, and potential consequences for your prospect. This process is not about the benefits of your offer. It's about activating people's Key Engagers: fear of loss, curious insecurities, competitiveness, and their strong desire to be a serious player. Only when you have gained the access you need—i.e., when you're in the meeting or conference you requested—should you shift your primary focus from the leverage you've created to the benefits of your offer.

2. Visualize the Circle of Leverage diagram as you carry out this step. Imagine your prospect huddled in the center, inside their circular fortress. Then imagine the power of each Leverage Point pressing on that fortress more and more from all sides, without letting up. Soon the walls begin to crumble, and your prospect has nowhere to turn.

You can make this vision a reality by systematically flushing out all of your prospect's Leverage Points, keeping careful, *written* track of exactly who has said and done what, and following up with everyone—time after time, if necessary—until you get clear responses to your request for access from everyone.

3. Everyone has their own agenda. Each person who receives your request for access may very well view it differently, because each has their own motives, fears, hopes, desires, etc. As a result, the person you initially targeted as your prospect may say, "No, thank you, we don't need to meet," but someone else in the organization (usually a Leverage Point) may respond, "Come on in and talk with us." *This happens all the time.* Be flexible and willing to be bounced around until you're in.

4. Never disguise or sugar-coat what you are doing. Make it clear at all times exactly what you want—either access, a referral to the proper decision maker, or a clear no. All of this is so unexpected and refreshing for people that many of them immediately begin to trust you, become more attentive, or do their best to help you. They know they're being prospected, so say so!

5. Remind everyone, over and over, of the other recipients of your communication. In every follow-up call, mention all the other people who have gotten your letter and explain that you'll be (or are already) following up with *everyone*. This keeps your leverage fresh and consistent, and keeps your prospects and Leverage Points from hiding from you.

Also remind people of any of their competitors you deal with, have dealt with in the past, or will be dealing with shortly. Mention the specific person as well as the organization—"You know, I'm going to be in Denver next week meeting with Felicia Gonzales about our services. She's your counterpart at The Hoskins Group; maybe you know her." Often this doubles your leverage.

If you haven't booked any appointments or conferences yet, you can still apply some general leverage by saying something like this: "I plan on meeting with other key executives in your industry with your level of responsibility over the next few weeks and am currently in touch with them" (i.e., you've requested access from them).

6. Leave the polite but clear impression that you can't be stopped until your ultimate prospect responds to your request for access with a definite yes or no. Don't say this outright, of course. Let it be implicit in your manner by remaining 100 percent polite, firm, and straightforward about the fact that all you want is a response to your request. Yes or no!

7. It is impossible to predict which Leverage Point will provide the most powerful leverage against your ultimate prospect. That's why it's so important to continue flushing out everyone until you know who your ultimate prospect is.

8. Don't be surprised or disappointed if your letter is routed and then rerouted, or if two copies of your letter get routed to two different people. Flushing out your prospect sometimes means being bounced around from one person to another. *This is good news!* It means you are getting closer to the person or group that's your real prospect.

Sometimes the people you've approached aren't sure themselves who the right decision maker is—especially if your offer is unusual or the organization hasn't considered anything like it before. Let yourself be bounced around; if you keep your leverage fresh and consistent, eventually you'll reach your real prospect.

9. If you are ultimately referred to someone in the organization who's lower down than anyone you approached, that's okay. Because that referral comes from above, the person you've been directed to will probably take it very seriously.

10. The "appropriate person" is not always the appropriate person. Sometimes there will be genuine disagreement—or outright confusion—about who should handle your request. At other times, people may "refer" you to someone else just to duck their responsibility or get rid of you. *Never get angry at this or let it drive you crazy.* Remember, it's just a game—and, often, a classic case of avoidance, lack of concern, lack of leadership, etc. Continue applying leverage and flushing out people in the organization—following up with the people who gave you bogus or incorrect referrals, if necessary—until you've located the most promising person or group to present your offer to. Then *you* decide whether it's worth your time to continue.

Sometimes—and unfortunately this is happening more and more often—someone who claims to be the decision maker in fact has no such power. There's nothing you can do to prevent this. The C.O.L. is not a lie detector.

11. Expect some contradictory information and contradicting levels of interest, particularly in the early stages of gaining access. These mixed signals are normal. Remember that each organization, prospect, and Leverage Point is in a constant state of flux and change, and it sometimes takes a while for everyone involved to sort out if there is interest, who is interested, and how to proceed. Simply continue following up by phone until you get the access you need—or a "no, thank you."

12. Let people know what others in their organization have said to you. Don't give anyone the chance to keep secrets, act in a vacuum, or say one thing and do another. Be simultaneously frank, polite, and Columbo-like: "I appreciate your letting me know that Diane's the person I should be talking with. But maybe you can help me resolve some confusion, because both Nelson Modleski and Martha Green told me that *you're* the one who makes decisions on these matters." This keeps everybody honest *and* keeps your leverage firm and consistent.

13. If your ultimate prospect turns out to be a task force,

committee, or other group, treat all members of the group as prospects. If you're routed to the group's chairperson or official liaison, that's fine. But ask this person where the real decision-making authority lies. If the group will make a joint decision, try to schedule a meeting or conference with the whole group, not just one member.

Often task forces and committees don't make final decisions, but merely make recommendations to someone higher up. You'll have to make a case-by-case decision whether to deal with a committee or try to get in the door of whomever it reports to. (I've done it both ways.) It all depends on how seriously the committee's recommendations are likely to be taken, whether it will recommend one or several finalists, etc.

14. For a variety of reasons, a small percentage of all messages go astray. If someone tells you they didn't get your initial communication, forward another (normally by fax) as soon as possible.

A Sample Follow-up Call

While every follow-up call you make will go differently, here's how a typical conversation might proceed:

"Hi. Is this Olivia, Mark's secretary?"

"Yes it is."

"Good. This is Corrine Martineau. I head up the marketing division for GHI Corporation, and I'm following up on a letter I sent to Mark on March thirty-first, which probably landed in your office on April second. I'm hoping you saw it. I also sent copies of this letter to _____, _____, _____, and _____ at your company. Do you have time to take my name and number so I can tell you what this regards?"

"Certainly. It's Corrine Martineau?"

"That's right. Martineau. [Spell it.] My number in Kansas City is 800-555-5555. Actually, Olivia, I don't need to speak with Mark, if you can answer a couple of quick questions for me. You may remember the letter. It explained how GHI helps large corporations and nonprofits trim their accounting costs. I requested a twenty-minute meeting with Mark later on in the month. Have you seen the letter? I'm hoping you did."

"Oh, yes." (Laughs.) "In fact, it's been creating a bit of a buzz around here with the different people who got copies."

"Great. Do you know if Mark has read it yet?"

"I'm sure he must have. He and a couple of other people have been talking about it."

"Do you know if he still has the letter, or has he routed it to someone else?"

"No, it's still here, but I don't think he's made any decision on it yet."

"As I said, I don't need to talk with him directly so long as I can work with you. Let me fill you in on when I'll be in town, so if he's interested in meeting, he can pick a convenient time. You're the one who controls his appointment calendar and schedule, aren't you?"

"Well, he has the final say, but I usually do the actual arranging."

"I'll be in town from the tenth through the twelfth, meeting with people such as Mark at a number of companies in your industry. In fact, some are your competitors. It looks like the morning of the eleventh or twelfth would work. If he'd like to meet, any twenty-minute period during those times works well for me. Is he even in town during those days?"

"He'll be gone the twelfth, but otherwise it looks like he'll be here."

"Good. What I'd like to know, then, is whether he's interested in meeting. I'll call you back on Wednesday afternoon to find out if he wants to meet and when the best time for him is. If you find out before then, or if he routes my letter to someone else, would you please call my 800 number and leave me a voice mail message as to how you want me to proceed?"

"I'd be happy to do that."

"Thank you. One last thing. Since I've sent copies of the letter to _____, _____, _____, and _____, and the letter promises that I will follow up, I'll be calling those four people to get their responses as well. Thanks again for your time and your help. Bye."

Sample C.O.L. Forms

As you go through the flushing-out process, your mental picture of the targeted organization may change. The person you thought was

218

your prospect may turn out not to be, and one or more new potential prospects may emerge. Reporting relationships, job titles, and people's responsibilities may not be exactly what you expected. Certain people may be out of the country, or away on maternity leave, or no longer with the company. Your letter may be routed first to one person, then another.

You must *keep track of all of this movement* if you are to stay on top of the game and keep your leverage fresh and consistent. The best way to do this is to make detailed notes on your C.O.L. form (from page 90 or 156). Write yourself messages, draw arrows and circles— whatever enables you *at a glance* to keep track of what's going on with your letter, who is still involved with it, whom you've called and when, what transpired in each conversation, and whom you still need to follow up with. Keep this form near the phone for easy reference.

On pages 220–222 are some sample C.O.L. forms as they might look during this Execution Step.

In Summary:

- The C.O.L. often enables you to skip the entire process of talking your way in. Instead, it quickly delivers either the access you desire or a firm and unequivocal no.

- With the C.O.L., you normally do not attempt to get your prospects or Leverage Points on the phone to talk about the benefits of your offer. You simply follow up with the assistants of every recipient of your letter to find out:

  1. Did the prospect or Leverage Point see and read your communication? *Yes or no.*

  2. Do they wish to grant your request for access? *Yes or no.*

  3. Did they or their assistant route your letter to someone else? If so, find out the details:
     a. The name and title of that person.
     b. Their relationship to the original recipient of your letter.
     c. If the new recipient is aware that the letter is coming.

219

VWX Collection Agency

(For a job interview as a collector)

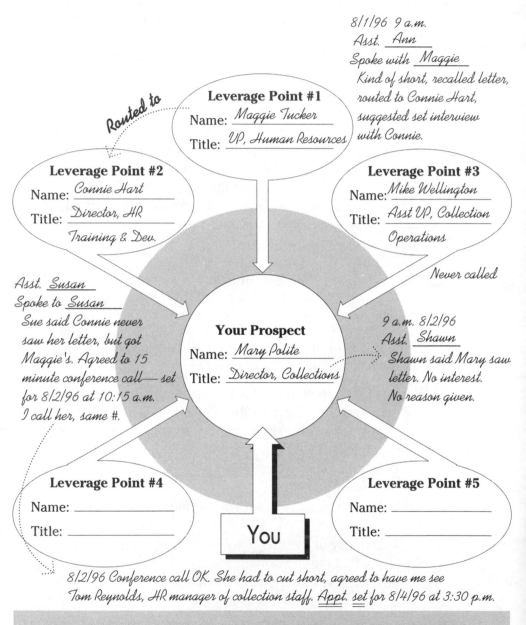

8/1/96 9 a.m.
Asst. _Ann_
Spoke with _Maggie_
Kind of short, recalled letter,
routed to Connie Hart,
suggested set interview
with Connie.

Routed to

Leverage Point #1
Name: _Maggie Tucker_
Title: _VP, Human Resources_

Leverage Point #2
Name: _Connie Hart_
Title: _Director, HR_
Training & Dev.

Leverage Point #3
Name: _Mike Wellington_
Title: _Asst VP, Collection_
Operations

Never called

Asst. _Susan_
Spoke to _Susan_
Sue said Connie never
saw her letter, but got
Maggie's. Agreed to 15
minute conference call— set
for 8/2/96 at 10:15 a.m.
I call her, same #.

Your Prospect
Name: _Mary Polite_
Title: _Director, Collections_

9 a.m. 8/2/96
Asst. _Shawn_
Shawn said Mary saw
letter. No interest.
No reason given.

Leverage Point #4
Name: _____
Title: _____

You

Leverage Point #5
Name: _____
Title: _____

8/2/96 Conference call OK. She had to cut short, agreed to have me see
Tom Reynolds, HR manager of collection staff. Appt. set for 8/4/96 at 3:30 p.m.

The Leverage You Have Created Gets You in the Door

EFG Computer Company

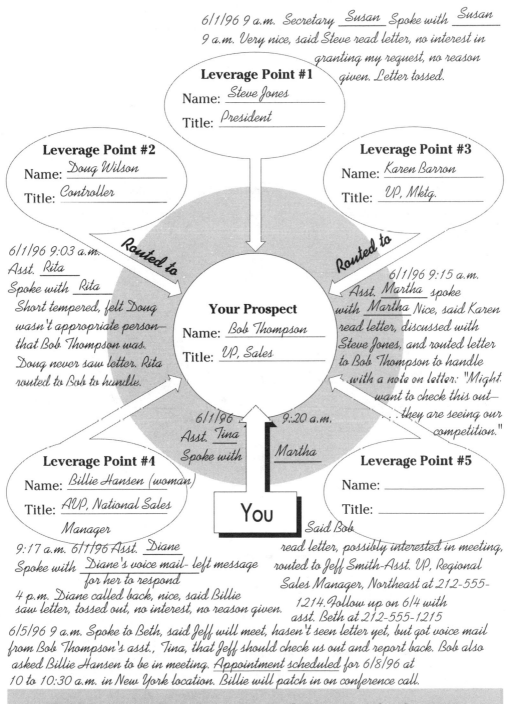

6/1/96 9 a.m. Secretary _Susan_ Spoke with _Susan_
9 a.m. Very nice, said Steve read letter, no interest in
granting my request, no reason
given. Letter tossed.

Leverage Point #1
Name: _Steve Jones_
Title: _President_

Leverage Point #2
Name: _Doug Wilson_
Title: _Controller_

Leverage Point #3
Name: _Karen Barron_
Title: _VP, Mktg._

Routed to

Routed to

6/1/96 9:03 a.m.
Asst. _Rita_
Spoke with _Rita_
Short tempered, felt Doug
wasn't appropriate person—
that Bob Thompson was.
Doug never saw letter. Rita
routed to Bob to handle.

Your Prospect
Name: _Bob Thompson_
Title: _VP, Sales_

6/1/96 9:15 a.m.
Asst. _Martha_ spoke
with _Martha_ Nice, said Karen
read letter, discussed with
Steve Jones, and routed letter
to Bob Thompson to handle
with a note on letter: "Might
want to check this out—
. . . they are seeing our
competition."

6/1/86 9:20 a.m.
Asst. _Tina_
Spoke with _Martha_

You

Leverage Point #4
Name: _Billie Hansen (woman)_
Title: _AVP, National Sales Manager_

Leverage Point #5
Name: _____
Title: _____

Said Bob
read letter, possibly interested in meeting,
routed to Jeff Smith-Asst. VP, Regional
Sales Manager, Northeast at 212-555-
1214. Follow up on 6/4 with
asst. Beth at 212-555-1215

9:17 a.m. 6/1/96 Asst. _Diane_
Spoke with _Diane's voice mail- left message for her to respond_
4 p.m. Diane called back, nice, said Billie
saw letter, tossed out, no interest, no reason given.

6/5/96 9 a.m. Spoke to Beth, said Jeff will meet, hasn't seen letter yet, but got voice mail
from Bob Thompson's asst., Tina, that Jeff should check us out and report back. Bob also
asked Billie Hansen to be in meeting. _Appointment_ scheduled for 6/8/96 at
10 to 10:30 a.m. in New York location. Billie will patch in on conference call.

The Leverage You Have Created Gets You in the Door

Con Edna Utility Co.

7/1/96 9 a.m. Asst. _Barb_ Spoke with _Sue_ Barb out all week on cruise. Sue saw letter, nice, said Michael read letter, routed it to Kevin Brown to deal with.

Leverage Point #1
Name: _Michael Stevens_
Title: _VP, Law_

Leverage Point #2
Name: _Bill Thomas_
Title: _Asst. VP, Governmental Affairs_

Routed to

Leverage Point #3
Name: _Don Bennet_
Title: _General Counsel_

Routed to

Routed to

7/1/96
9:30 a.m.
Asst. _Bethanne_
Spoke to: _Bethanne_
very rushed, rude, said Bill saw letter, routed to Don Bennet, felt he's the right guy to handle, should see it today.

Your Prospect
Name: _Kevin Brown_
Title: _Asst. General Counsel, Litigation_

7/1/96
10:10 a.m.
Asst. _Sue_
Spoke to Sue
said Don never saw letter, he's out of country for 3 weeks. She forwarded Bill Thomas's copy to Kevin Brown with a note that Michael Stevens felt it might be something to look into

Leverage Point #4
Name: _____
Title: _____

You

Leverage Point #5
Name: _____
Title: _____

7/1/96 Asst. _Carol_ 10:15 a.m. Spoke to Carol
Very nice. Said Kevin, has 3 letters: his, Michael Stevens', and Bennet's. _Will meet_ on 7/3/96 at 9:30 to 10 a.m. at headquarters location.
Appt. set. Will also pull in Bill Thomas, AVP, Gov. Affairs, and Jim Fox, Sr. Managing Attorney & Director of Governmental Affairs.

The Leverage You Have Created Gets You in the Door

     d.   When they should receive it.

     e.   If a message was sent along with it.

     f.   Who did the routing—the original recipient or their assistant?

- Allow one to two business days after your communication has landed before making your follow-up calls to flush out each recipient's response.

- Simultaneously, call the assistant of every one of your Leverage Points, in order of highest to lowest rank. Call your prospect's assistant last.

- If talking to an assistant is not possible, select the next best option:

  —Your prospect or Leverage Point's voice mail.

  —Their assistant's voice mail.

  —The secretary or receptionist for the department, floor, or whole organization.

  —A substitute, temporary, or floating assistant.

  —The prospect or Leverage Point themselves.

  —Voice mail for the entire organization, division, or unit.

- In every follow-up call, remind everyone over and over of the other individuals who have received the same correspondence. This keeps your leverage fresh and each recipient engaged.

- Leave the polite but clear impression that you can't be stopped until your ultimate prospect responds to your request for access with a definite yes or no.

- Avoid discussing your offer on the phone. If you're asked about it point-blank, briefly explain its key net benefits and your positioning statement, then press for the appointment or conference you've requested. As necessary, dance, sponge, and reiterate according to the guidelines in Chapter 26.

- If your letter has been routed to someone else, add them to your list of people to follow up with, flushing them out in the same manner.

- Keep track of who you talk to, when you talk with them, and what you learn on your C.O.L. forms. Fill in any other useful information you obtain on your Prospect Portraits and Organization Profiles.

- Continue following up by phone, flushing out all responses, until your real prospect bubbles to the surface and responds to your request for access.

- If your ultimate prospect turns out to be a task force, committee, or other group, treat all members of the group as prospects.

- When a prospect or Leverage Point grants your request for access, immediately book the appointment or conference and stop making follow-up calls to anyone else in the organization. The C.O.L. delivered. You're in!

- If you get a clear no, graciously thank the person and hang up. However, continue to follow up with every other person your letter went to in the organization until you have a response from all recipients—unless it's very clear that they've all said no as a group.

- If someone does not respond to your letter or three follow-up calls, write them off and focus your attention on other people in the organization.

Twenty-Six

Execution Step #3:
Dance, Sponge, and Reiterate

The Persuasive Art

This step is for those times when you make a follow-up call and your prospect or Leverage Point picks up the phone—or when *you* pick up the phone to discover a prospect or Leverage Point on the line. It's also for those instances when someone insists on speaking with you before deciding whether to grant your request for access.

In any of these situations, you've got to demonstrate to your prospect or Leverage Point that it's to their benefit to grant the appointment or conference you've requested. At the same time, you must neither explain too much about your offer nor frustrate your prospect or Leverage Point by not explaining enough. You need to listen carefully, make snap decisions, and walk a tightrope between withholding and revealing too much information.

If this sounds like a delicate situation, you're right.

This step is the toughest to explain and teach, because it's more of an art than a science. It has everything to do with being flexible, agile, and willing to tactfully bounce back, until you're granted access—or until it's evident that it's time to stop pushing.

Some people are naturally more talented in using this step than others, but everyone gets better at it with experience. It's like learning to ride a bicycle: You practice, fail, practice some more, eventually succeed, and then continue to practice until the whole process comes naturally. Eventually, with experience, you'll become an expert.

Let's define the three activities this chapter focuses on:

Dancing is instantly adapting to another person's conversational and emotional rhythms—similar to what Tony Robbins refers to as matching and mirroring.

Sponging is soaking up key information from them, while searching for their most important need or goal.

Reiterating is restating key information they've given you and asking for details and clarification, to keep your prospects and Leverage Points honest.

Usually your conversation will lead you into these activities in the above sequence. As you continue listening and talking, however, you'll often find yourself doing all three at once—just as, in riding a bicycle, you're often pedaling, steering, and shifting gears simultaneously.

Dancing

Some people talk slowly and methodically; others speak very quickly and jump from subject to subject; still others pause frequently, think for a moment, then continue. Everyone has their own unique conversational style and rhythm—including you.

Furthermore, everyone's speech has an emotional component as well. Some people speak loudly and resonantly; others mumble. Some people's voices are naturally cheery and emphatic, while others' are restrained and even. Imagine Bob Dole and Jesse Jackson each reading the Gettysburg Address. There's a big difference, isn't there?

Every conversation is a dance. In order to dance smoothly with any prospect or Leverage Point, so they become *instantly* comfortable with you on the phone, you've got to mirror their conversational patterns. They may be rocking out, or they may be waltzing—but whatever dance they're doing, you need to observe it, learn it, and do it yourself if you want to build comfort and generate trust and rapport.

You must start doing the same dance *quickly*, because your prospect or Leverage Point is already dancing on the dance floor—and they're not likely to give you much time to get in step.

Dancing is not about developing a strong, clearly recognizable conversational style. It's about being able to adapt to the style of whomever you're talking with. It's about following, not leading.

Dancing means mirroring the other person's:

- General approach

- Conversational rhythm

- Level of emotion

- Attitude

- Pace

- Rhythm

- Level of formality

- Volume

If your prospect cuts straight to the chase and, without introduction, immediately wants to know the answers to several questions, fire back answers that are brief, sharp, and to the point. If they're more laid back and ask more general questions ("So, can you tell me about the technical support you provide?"), speak more slowly and give more general answers. Whatever they do, you do. (Stop short of mimicking their accent, of course.)

The more you mirror another person's conversational and emotional style, the more comfortable and in synch with you they will feel, and the easier it will be for them to listen to and understand you. Ultimately, the better you match their steps, the more positive they are likely to feel about you and your offer.

Conversational dancing can be learned, just like regular dancing.

Practice it at home by mirroring the conversational styles of friends and family members.

Sponging

Once you're in synch with your prospect or Leverage Point, you're in an ideal position to hone in on some need or goal they have—either personal or professional. This goal may or may not be relevant to their entire organization. Sponging involves diligently uncovering this need or goal by asking focused questions.

You want your dancing partner to open up about their situation, the specific challenges they're dealing with, their worries and concerns, and so on. You're looking for a crack in their armor, or a common bond that makes them think, "Hey, wait a minute. Maybe I should pay attention here."

An excellent place to begin sponging is by asking about a problem your offer solves or addresses. For instance: "People in your position tell me they have trouble maintaining the right levels of inventory. Is this your situation?" You've predicted that your prospect's organization has this problem, and if it does, you've got the perfect solution. But here's the sweet part: If this area *isn't* a problem, there's a good chance the person will reply, "Actually, we've got that pretty well under control. It's _____ that's our real dilemma." Suddenly, they've revealed a problem that (perhaps) your offer can address—and they've provided a handle you can use to help get in their door.

Often the answers to one question lead to others. Keep asking more questions until you find out what that person's important needs or goals are. Then explain, briefly, how your offer can help meet that need or goal. Finally, of course, remind them of the leverage you've created: "As you know, my initial letter went out to _____, _____, and _____ as well, and I'm in the process of following up with them, as the letter states. Do you wish to meet for twenty minutes, or would you prefer I meet with one of the other people?"

One of my favorite—and most successful—forms of sponging is qualifying my prospect or Leverage Point. I especially like to use this when the person on the other end of the line makes a point of showing off their power or wants me to grovel a bit because they've graced me with their presence. This type of person *expects* me to start blasting away about the benefits of my offer, or promising just about anything to get in their door. It's what they're used to.

Instead, *I do the exact opposite* of what they expect. I draw them out by moving *away* from trying to convince them to see me: "Rodney, in my experience companies like yours are usually excellent prospects for us because we can usually help them to _____ and _____. But from what you've told me so far, I'm not sure yet if we can help you. However, if I can just ask you a few quick questions, I'll be able to determine whether it would be a good idea for us to get together or not." Then I start sponging.

This usually works like a charm. First, I've disarmed Rodney by not pushing for access—and by suggesting that if I can't help his organization significantly, I'll go away. At this point, he actually begins helping me qualify him. Second, by demonstrating that I'm more concerned with *his* needs than with forcing my way in, I help him trust me more. Third, I've created the perfect context for asking questions—and for using the answers to those questions to get the access I need. Fourth, I've created a power shift from him to me. Rodney no longer perceives me as a peddler or schmoozer, someone who just wants to worm his way in, but as a helper, someone who realizes that wasting people's time benefits nobody. Fifth, if I can help Rodney's organization, I can offer him a win-win outcome by letting him know that I've qualified him: "Rodney, based on what you've told me, it sounds as if we can really help you, and therefore I'd like to meet for twenty minutes to present exactly how our product can benefit your company in these two areas: _____ and _____." Then I remind Rodney of the leverage I've created by mentioning the names of the other people in his organization I'm following up with.

At this point Rodney is surrounded. Between my having qualified him as a good prospect and the leverage bearing down on him, he's going to have a tough time *not* letting me in.

Reiterating

Once your prospect or Leverage Point has given you some pertinent information, repeat that information back and ask for clarification or details. This helps you in two ways: First, it creates a clearer picture of their needs, goals, and things they respond to; second, it uncovers the fluff—the pieces of their story that are exaggerated, or otherwise less than accurate and honest. Either way, you can use this information to further qualify them, apply more leverage, or both.

Here's an example. In 1994, I worked for a firm that sold document-processing services to the general counsels (translation: chief lawyers) of Fortune 500 companies. I decided to prospect one particular very large holding company. My initial prospect was the General Counsel and Senior Vice President of the whole firm. I also knew from my research that the General Counsel of its securities division (the company had more than a dozen divisions) would be a good prospect as well. I decided to focus on the General Counsel of the holding company for starters and see where the C.O.L. process led me.

I wrote my C.O.L. letter, mailed it to the General Counsel of the company and his Leverage Points, and made some follow-up calls. When I called his executive assistant, she was at lunch, and he picked up the phone. We talked for a bit, and I danced, sponged, and reiterated. Soon, however, he was ready to end the call: "We already have what it seems like your service offers, Michael. In fact, we've been working for the past two years with an outside consulting firm to help us institute an enterprise-wide solution."

There it was—the potential crack in his corporate armor! I wasn't *sure* a crack was there, but I thought there *might be*, simply because in a company as large as his, the right hand rarely knows (or cares) what the left hand is doing. I'd done my homework, and I'd kept careful track of where my letters had been routed, so I knew exactly what leverage to apply. I said, "Jim, if you've already got an enterprise-wide solution that works for you, there's no need for us to talk further, because it sounds as though you've got things nailed perfectly.

"One last question, though, to make sure I understand. To me, enterprise-wide means exactly that—your solution is being used enterprise-wide in the General Counsels' offices of all of your divisions. So I can assume, then, that _____, the Senior Vice President and General Counsel of your securities division, already knows about this solution and is using it, too. Correct?"

What followed was probably the longest pause in the history of telephone communications.

Finally, he spoke—a bit curtly. "_____ (the General Counsel) in our securities division doesn't know anything about what we're doing over here at corporate with our enterprise-wide solution. He's not a part of what we are doing. I don't know what the hell they're doing over there. That's separate from us."

I said, "Great. Since your needs sound like they are taken care of, and since _____'s needs are probably not going to be addressed by your 'enterprise-wide' solution, I'll put in a call to him. In fact, your president has routed my letter to him and directed me to call him to set up a meeting." (Which of course was true. I used it as my trump card.)

There was nothing Jim could say or do to block me. I placed the call to the Senior Vice President and General Counsel of the securities division and booked the appointment.

When I arrived in New York for the appointment, six people were there to listen to my presentation: two senior vice presidents, two vice presidents, and two senior managing attorneys in charge of litigation.

As you can see, when reiterating is combined with leverage, it helps keep everyone honest, and paying attention.

The key to reiterating is mirroring your prospect's biggest need, goal, or problem with your offer's single biggest benefit or point of difference. Repeat their problem; then explain that your benefit or point of difference is their solution. Repeat their goal; then explain that this benefit or difference will help them attain it. Reiterate their concern or fear; then reassure them that your benefits address it

Sometimes, by focusing on your key points of difference, you demonstrate that you can help *in a way none of your competitors can.* Add some leverage to this, and you've got a recipe for gaining access that few people can say no to.

Reiterating can also mean leading your prospect or Leverage Point through a step-by-step logical process in which your key point of difference is the centerpiece. In this process you review in detail where they are now, then lead them to the conclusion that it's in their best interest to grant you access. (I led you through a similar process of review at the beginning of Chapter 25.)

Do the following:

1. Repeat your prospect's own goals, objectives, needs, concerns, etc., as they've been communicated to you.

2. Restate the names of all your competitors they've looked at, or are currently considering.

3. <u>Review the key benefits each competitor's offer provides.</u> (If you can't do this quickly and fluently, you're dead. But you'll be able to do it with ease, simply by reading from the Competition Profile you filled out.)

4. <u>Reiterate your one or two biggest points of difference</u>, mirroring their biggest goals, needs, concerns, etc. If appropriate, mention your positioning statement.

5. <u>Get their agreement that this is what they're trying to achieve.</u> ("Have I heard you correctly, that your biggest concern is getting your products to your customers faster and more reliably?")

6. <u>Remind them that your offer could make them a big hero.</u> "It sounds to me that if you can find a way to get those products out faster and more safely, you and your company both stand to win." If you like, also paint a quick verbal picture of how much better off they and their organization will be once they've accepted your offer: "It'll be nice to tell your customers, 'We'll have it in your warehouse in three days—no ifs, ands, buts, or damage.' "

7. <u>State the benefits of granting you access</u> (*not* the benefits of your offer) from Chapter 21. For instance: "Julia, I know you want to make an informed decision so you can generate the best results for you and your company. I know you want to feel secure that you've looked at all the important options, so you can be 100 percent comfortable with whatever decision you make. Once we've met for twenty minutes, you'll have all the information you need to make the best decision and stand behind it."

8. <u>Mention the leverage you've brought to bear on them</u>, both from within their organization and outside it. "Julia, I know this problem is important. It's precisely the same situation we've helped other companies with, such as _____, _____, _____, and _____. In fact, next week I'll be speaking with other firms in your industry about the same thing, including VWX Corporation and RST Partners. Do you know Tom Winkelman at RST?" (Pause for answer.) "I'll also be following up with _____, _____, and _____ in your company, since I've sent them letters as well and promised them I'd follow up to find out what level of interest they have and whom I should be dealing with."

9. <u>Repeat your request for access</u> in a simple, direct question ("Can we schedule a twenty-minute meeting?"). At this point, the question speaks volumes—and positively oozes leverage.

Please note that *at no time* in this process have you launched into any kind of pitch about your incredible, earth-shakingly-wonderful offer. Instead, you've focused on your prospect or Leverage Point's situation, on *their* concerns, and on the leverage you've brought to bear on them. Your actual discussion of your offer has been limited to its key benefits and points of difference. *That's all you need.* Remember, if you say much more, you run the risk of getting sucked into making a mini-presentation, and you'll lose leverage.

Using Your Other Firepower

As you dance, sponge, and reiterate, feel free to bring to your prospect or Leverage Point's attention any other information that will make you more credible or impressive in their eyes. These items might include:

- Connections or referrals (assuming you've checked them out first)

- References or testimonials

- A good track record in the industry

- Credentials, background, or experience

- A well-known name behind you

- An impressive title or position of responsibility

- Case histories of how you or your organization have helped similar organizations

- "Credibility bricks": pieces of extremely favorable information that you know will interest the person (see page 110)

As you can see, this Execution Step involves putting together all the skills and techniques you've developed so far. That's why this step is often the most fun—and the one that usually takes the most practice to master.

In Summary:

- *Dancing* is adapting to and mirroring another person's conversational and emotional rhythms, matching their general approach, level of emotion, attitude, pace, level of formality, and volume.

- The more you mirror the other person's conversational style, the more comfortable they will feel, and the more receptive they will be.

- *Sponging* is soaking up key information and details—digging for your prospect's most important need or goal by asking focused questions.

- *Reiterating* is restating key information and asking for clarification and details. This gets your prospect to reveal their needs and goals in more depth. It also uncovers inaccuracies and exaggerations.

- The key to reiterating is mirroring your prospect's biggest need, goal, or problem with your offer's biggest point(s) of difference or key benefits. This not only shows that your offer can help, but also demonstrates that it can do so in a way none of your competitors' offers can.

- As you dance, sponge, and reiterate, mention any other information that will make you more credible or impressive in your prospect or Leverage Point's eyes.

Twenty-Seven

Execution Step #4:
Align and Champion Your Offer

You've got your prospect on the phone—and you've got them intrigued. They've asked you some questions about your offer, which you've answered. Maybe you've sent them some material by mail as well. You've danced, sponged, and reiterated to the best of your ability—maybe over the course of several phone calls. You've repeated the key benefits of your offer and your positioning statement. And you've reminded them of all the leverage you've surrounded them with.

But when you ask to schedule an appointment, they still won't say yes. They want to know more. "Tell me more about _____." "Can you send me any other material by mail?" "Give me your presentation right now, over the phone. You've got me now, so let me have it."

It's very tempting, I know, to respond to these requests, since the prospect is clearly interested, and since you're so close to getting in. *But in the game of access, close doesn't count!* You either get in or you don't. And the fact is that the more information you give out over the phone or through the mail—no matter how fantastic your offer is— the more you *undermine* your chances of getting in. Furthermore, the closer you are to getting access, the more you can hurt yourself by saying too much.

Remember, whether your prospect admits it or not, most of the time they are looking for a reason to say no to your offer and to your request for access. *Don't give them that chance.*

You're in a double bind here. On the one hand, your prospect has made it clear that your leverage alone is not going to get you in their door—they need to be convinced about the merits of your offer as well. On the other, the more information you provide, the more vulnerable you become. What do you do?

Very briefly, place the focus on your offer. In no more than a few sentences:

1. Tactfully remind your prospect of the goals and/or mission of their organization. If you like, frame this as a question: "My understanding is that your company's mission is to provide the highest quality custom-designed landscaping services for large businesses. Is that correct?"

2. Explain that your offer is expressly designed to help organizations such as theirs reach their goals or fulfill their missions. "Our company exists to help organizations such as yours. That's *our* mission." You are thus aligning your offer with their higher cause.

3. Explain—in, at most, three or four sentences—how the net benefits of your offer can help their organization do what it does *faster, cheaper, and/or better.*

All told, this micro-presentation should take no more than one to two minutes.

This approach has proven highly effective in convincing prospects to finally get off the fence and open their doors, while actually giving them very little new information. Instead, it gives them a new *perspective* on the offer and the person making it.

This step works for two reasons.

First, when you align your offer with the general goals of your prospect's organization, you force them out of their own agenda and back into the organization's. They either have to let you in or say, in effect, "I really don't care whether you help my organization or not." Even if they really *don't* care, they certainly don't want to broadcast that fact to others who have power over them. And, as you've told them, you plan to call some of those very people shortly. Think of how it will look when you tell them (in so many words), "Yes, I spoke with _____ about how our service can help your company reach its goals faster, better, and cheaper, but she made it clear that those goals weren't important to her." Some prospects won't like this, but they'll have a hard time fighting it.

Second, even the most inattentive, suspicious, or arrogant prospect can understand the concepts of faster, cheaper, and better. Sometimes, in fact, those are the *only* concepts that finally get them to take your offer seriously. Wouldn't *you* want to know more about an answering machine or a VCR or a computer that does everything your current one does—but faster, cheaper, or better?

By blanketing your offer in the goals and objectives of your prospect's *organization*, and by stressing the most basic and obvious of benefits, you give your prospect virtually no choice but to grant you access. That's why when all else fails, this step often provides the final chunk of leverage that gets you the access you need.

In Summary:

- The more information you give out over the phone, the more you undermine your chances of getting in.

- If your prospect insists on finding out more about your offer, do the following:

  1. Tactfully remind them of the goals and/or mission of their organization.
  2. Explain that your offer is expressly designed to help orga-

nizations such as theirs reach their goals or fulfill their missions.

3. Explain in sound-bite fashion how your offer can help their organization do what it does *faster, cheaper, and/or better.*

Twenty-Eight

Execution Step #5:
Open Their Door

This step is the easiest of all—and the easiest to overlook.

Imagine you're on the phone with a prospect, a Leverage Point, or an assistant. You've danced, sponged, and reiterated, championed and aligned your offer, and reminded them of the leverage you've created. You can almost hear their resistance crumbling.

But you still need to do one more thing: *Stop* talking about your offer and ask for access. Ask for the meeting or conference you requested in your earlier communication.

I've made this a separate step because people new to the C.O.L. sometimes forget to do it. They carry out the first fourteen steps pretty well, but then they sit back and expect their prospects to *offer* them access. That's a mistake.

While people do open their doors without prompting once in a while, it's definitely not the norm. (If it were, you wouldn't need this book!) Most of the time in this world, if you don't ask for something—access or anything else—you don't get it.

So, once you've said everything else you need to say, don't ramble on. Make a clear, specific request for access near the end of *every* phone call.

The simple question, "Can we schedule an appointment?," forces your prospect to respond with a yes, a no, or a request for more information. And when your question has all your combined leverage behind it, the answer is yes much of the time.

Congratulations! You've now learned all the essentials of a profoundly powerful system that can make a very real difference in your professional life—and perhaps in your personal life as well. You now have at hand a new philosophy and a basic tool set for gaining access to people faster, more effectively, at a higher level, and with less expense, so you can make more money, achieve greater results, and experience more success.

But please don't stop here. The rest of the book offers you concepts, approaches, and hands-on exercises that will enable you to use the C.O.L. even more effectively.

In Summary:

- Always make a clear, specific request for the access you need near the end of *every* phone call with a prospect, Leverage Point, or assistant. How can you expect to get in if you don't ask for access?

ADVANCED MOVES

Twenty-Nine

Turning Up the Heat

T o use the C.O.L. most effectively, it's important to create as much leverage as you can. In addition, however, you must remind people—tactfully—that it exists. Some examples:

"I'll be following up with _____, _____, and _____ within the next few days. As you know, I sent copies of my letter to them as well and promised each one I'd follow up by phone."

"We've had a good deal of success helping organizations such as yours, including _____, _____, _____, and _____ [their direct competitors]."

"The first week in November I will be in Providence and expect to meet with the senior executives of exactly your level of responsibility at a number of the key players in your business."

There are two situations, though, where you should throw tact out the window and wave your leverage directly—though politely—in people's faces.

1. <u>When someone powerful has referred you.</u> Let's say you've selected as one of your Leverage Points Marilyn Hall, the president of The UVW Company. When you follow up with her by phone, her secretary says, "Marilyn told me to direct you to Harvey Moore, who handles these matters." (Harvey is another of your Leverage Points.) You call Harvey's office, and, after introducing yourself, *immediately* say, "I've been directed to Harvey by Marilyn Hall." This gets Harvey's assistant to immediately sit up and take notice—and when Harvey gets the message, he does, too.

2. <u>When you've booked an appointment with a prospect or Leverage Point's counterpart in a competing firm.</u> Most people are quite interested when they learn that you've gotten in a counterpart's door. They're even more interested when you gain access to their *boss's* counterpart.

Imagine this scenario: You're prospecting the marketing directors of several large HMOs. You begin your follow-up calls with MNO Health Centers and are granted an appointment with Hakim Norton, head of marketing, later in the month. Now that you've secured one appointment, you have what I call an anchor. You immediately stop making follow-up calls to MNO and turn your attention to its competitors. In each call, after you ask the three standard questions about your letter, you say something like this: "Please let your boss know that I'll be meeting with Hakim Norton, the Vice President of Marketing for MNO Health Centers"—and any other people you have secured appointments with. "That might boost my credibility with him, since he may know Hakim, and it may affect his decision about meeting with me." (You *know* it will—they're direct competitors!)

It may seem ridiculous, but it's what works.

People respond to power. And when you trip their Key Engagers, sometimes they respond all the more when you present that power and it's in their faces.

I think you see where to go from here. As you call your other prospects and Leverage Points, mention Hakim every time. Then, once you get an appointment with one of his counterparts, mention *both* marketing directors in every follow-up call you make. Momentum begins to build.

Eventually this creates a domino effect. One more door swings

244

open, then another. Each time you book a meeting, your leverage builds—until your remaining prospects feel they have no choice but to grant you access. (Does this domino effect actually happen in real life? You bet it does—quite often, in fact. No one wants to be left out in the cold.)

Here's a useful variation on this theme: Once you've scheduled your first meeting or conference with someone powerful, get back in touch with the people you've already called, *even if you just talked with them half an hour ago.* Tell them politely that you have booked an appointment with one of their counterparts, and listen to them suddenly grow more interested.

Waving leverage in people's faces can be so effective that, in certain circumstances, you may want to use it on people who have already said no to you.

A few years ago I was prospecting the general counsels of some of the country's largest oil companies, including Conoco. My C.O.L. letter worked extremely well at many of these firms, and I was able to book several appointments. But at Conoco, my prospect, the Senior Vice President and General Counsel, simply wasn't interested—and told me so through his assistant. Since I had nothing to lose, I called the assistant back and said, "Since your boss doesn't know me, and because I don't have any credibility with him, would you please let him know that I already have scheduled appointments with the following people, most of whom he knows pretty well." Then I recited the names and titles of his direct counterparts and near-counterparts at Mobil, Pennzoil, Exxon, and four other large oil companies. I added, "I think it's important that he knows that I'm seeing people of exactly his level of responsibility and authority. That may affect his decision on whether he wishes to sit with me for half an hour."

Gutsy? Sure. Bold? I guess so. Effective? Absolutely. His assistant called back within hours and said, "Mr. _____ would be happy to see you," and the appointment was booked. Why? I'll never really know. Maybe he didn't want to look dumb, or miss out on something his competition might use against him.

The moral of this story: The more powerful your leverage, the more blatantly you can use it to your advantage.

In Summary:

- There are two situations in which you should throw tact out the window and blatantly (though politely) let people know of the leverage you've created: (1) when someone powerful has referred you; and (2) when you've booked an appointment with someone's counterpart (or someone even more powerful) in a competing firm.

- The more powerful your referral, the more directly you can use it to your advantage.

- Once you've scheduled a meeting or conference with someone powerful, you've got an anchor. Then promptly inform all your prospects and Leverage Points at their competing organizations about it. Make a special round of calls if necessary.

Thirty

The Art of Blitzing:
The Ultimate Leverage

A High-Risk, High-Payoff Option

Normally when you use the C.O.L., you focus on one prospect per organization. Up until now, all the examples and situations I've provided have been based on this single-prospect situation.

There may be times, however, when you have more than one prospect in a single organization—*and* an extremely urgent need to get in their doors. These situations may call for *blitzing*: using the C.O.L. at full throttle to open two or more simultaneous pockets of influence, thereby gaining access to two or more prospects at once.

If planned and executed correctly, blitzing can deliver outstanding results. However, blitzing is *strong* medicine. Like blitzing in football, it is bold, aggressive, and extremely potent. It should therefore be used *only* in very specific circumstances.

Never blitz an organization unless *all* of the following apply:

1. You are a salesperson, business owner, or key executive with a product, service, or concept to sell.

2. You are pursuing a very lucrative opportunity.

3. The organization you are prospecting is large or very large (it has at least three hundred to five hundred employees).

4. You've identified a separate prospect *in each of two (or more) different divisions* in that organization who can absolutely, clearly benefit from your offer.

5. Your prospects are senior-level management.

6. You are comfortable with the fact that some of the people you blitz may get irritated at you because blitzing is so bold and direct.

7. You are supremely confident in your offer and its ability to help your prospects.

Blitzing should *never* be used to obtain a job interview, an endorsement or testimonial, a donation of time or money, or an order for products or services that's less than quite substantial.

Furthermore, blitzing should be used *only* in these situations:

- You need immediate action.

- You need a bolt of lightning to make your prospect wake up and *want* to pay attention to you.

- You already got in the door and made your presentation, but your prospect(s) didn't really pay attention to you or take you seriously.

- All your other efforts to get in have failed.

- It may be your last chance to act before a decision is made.

- You have nothing to lose.

Blitzing only works *once* with any organization. It's like crying "wolf!" Cry "wolf" once and it instantly motivates people to at least pay attention to you. Cry "wolf" a second or third time and it works against you. People get irritated and learn to ignore you.

The Blitzing Process

In blitzing, you locate two or more prospects—one per division, subsidiary, or unit—within the same large organization. Then you select at least three Leverage Points *for each prospect* from within their division. Also select at least one Leverage Point who supervises people from both your prospects' divisions. This person will exert leverage on both of your prospects simultaneously.

Your goal is to obtain the access you need with someone in each division.

Follow the steps of the C.O.L. just as you normally would, with every prospect and Leverage Point receiving copies of your letter at once. To get people's attention, I *strongly* recommend that you send your letters by courier or Express Mail.

As always, your follow-up calls must also be as close to simultaneous as possible. When you call, let people know the names and titles of *everyone* who has received your letter—not just the people in their own division. You want to create a separate pocket of influence *and* a separate funneling effect within each division.

Once you've gotten in the door in one division, stop making follow-up calls to people within that division—but continue the process everywhere else. *Immediately* let every remaining prospect and Leverage Point know about the access you've already been granted in their sister division. Then keep following up until the C.O.L. process is complete.

A diagram of the blitzing process appears on page 250. This will give you a visual sense of the enormous leverage that two separate (but overlapping) pockets of influence can create.

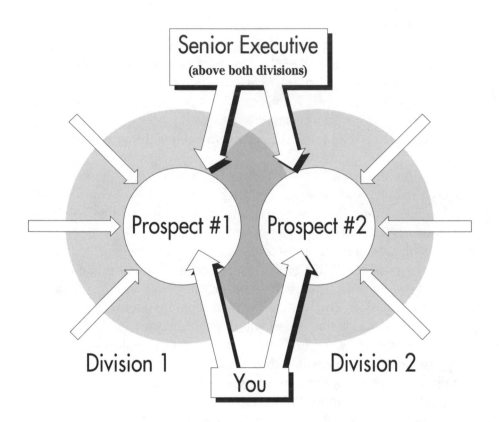

In Summary:

- Blitzing is using the C.O.L. at full throttle to simultaneously open multiple pockets of influence at two or more different divisions within the same large organization, with the goal of gaining access to a different prospect in each division.

- When you blitz, you identify two or more prospects—one per division, subsidiary, or unit—within the same large organization. Then you select at least three Leverage Points for each prospect within their own division, plus at least one Leverage Point who supervises people from *all* your prospects' divisions.

- Once you've gotten in the door of one division, stop making follow-up calls to people within the division, but continue the process everywhere else. *Immediately* let every remaining prospect and Leverage Point know of the access you've already obtained elsewhere in their organization.

- Blitzing can be very effective, but should be used only in *very* specific circumstances.

- *Never* use blitzing to obtain a job interview, an endorsement or testimonial, a donation of time or money, or an order for products or services that isn't for a substantial amount of money.

Thirty-One

Handling Misdirectors,
Turf Protectors, and
Bruised Egos

If you use the C.O.L. correctly, 95 percent of the people you contact won't have a problem with it. In fact, they won't notice a thing. They'll just respond automatically. Remember, the C.O.L. engages automatic responses that we've learned are normal and routine, since our birth.

While I've seen people be impressed, surprised, amazed, amused, intrigued, delighted, and even taken aback by the power of the System, only rarely has anyone responded to it as a personal threat.

But those who *do* take it personally may make it their business to get in your way, or your face, very quickly.

I call these people kingdom builders, turf protectors, or power hounds. Almost invariably, these are people interested in maintaining the status quo. They often take on the self-appointed role of the Rules Police. They're the ones who say, "We don't do it that way. You're supposed to do it *this* way." Typically, they are unhappy, insecure, small-minded, and attention-starved.

To turf protectors, the C.O.L. feels like a strong-arm tactic. But what's really going on is they're scared, because the System shakes the very ground they walk on. It directly challenges what little power they may have.

As you've probably guessed, it isn't just the C.O.L. that stirs up these people. All kinds of things—reorganization, downsizing, removal of the water cooler, replacement of Styrofoam coffee cups with paper ones—get their blood hot and send them into their "defend and attack" mode.

These people appear in organizations of all types, at all levels. I'm sure you've encountered your share of them already.

Some turf protectors are concerned solely with defending their own territory; others are fixated on "protecting" their bosses (maybe because they don't have much else to do). In still other cases, turf protectors are running interference *in direct opposition to the specific request of their bosses*. You'd be amazed at the number of secretaries who believe their primary duty is to keep potentially helpful people and information away from their superiors.

If you get a nasty letter from a turf protector, your course of action is clear and simple: File and forget it. And if the letter answers the questions on pages 202-203, great—you've got closure.

Most of the time, though, turf protectors want to rough you up a bit over the phone. **Here is a process that disarms these people and defuses their frustration.** At the same time it helps keep them honest, and often gets them to act on your behalf.

1. <u>Be courteous, attentive, kind, and strong throughout the conversation, no matter what the other person says or does.</u> This lets them feel safe and in control—and sends the message that you won't let them walk all over you. (I also try to leave a hint that I am unstoppable and can't be simply brushed off.)

2. <u>Let them gush.</u> Listen attentively, without interrupting. Let the turf protector go on about what the problem is, why they're upset, and whatever else they want. As appropriate, say things like "I see" and "Go on, please."

Once they've begun to run down, ask them politely to explain specifically what caused their problem or is making them unhappy. Then let them gush some more if they need to. Gather what information you can in the process; you may be able to use some of it as leverage later.

3. <u>Don't get defensive or begin a counterattack.</u> Either of these responses only makes the turf protector more adamant about what they're doing—and they could undermine your leverage. The goal is to try to understand their "concerns" as best you can.

If the turf protector gets truly abusive, simply hang up. If you feel it's appropriate, call their boss to report their actions. Otherwise, let them go. It's not worth your time.

4. <u>Qualify them.</u> When they've gotten their whole complaint off their chest, ask for their name, title, and relationship to the prospect you've targeted in their organization. They'll be more than happy to tell you, because it makes them feel more powerful.

5. <u>Find out if they're acting alone</u>—that is, if they're calling on their own behalf, or at the request of some other person or group. If they're not one of your prospects or Leverage Points, ask how they found out about you.

As you'll discover, turf protectors usually act alone, even though they may initially invoke the names of others ("Here at the New Products Division, we don't appreciate . . ." "Everyone here in the Columbus office is unhappy about . . .").

As you'll also discover, the higher up you go in any hierarchy, the more confident people are and the less likely they are to get their noses out of joint when you use the C.O.L.

6. <u>Reiterate the main complaint.</u> "I want to make sure I understand you and haven't misinterpreted anything. You're upset because . . ." This lets them know that you've been listening and that you understand.

7. <u>Remember what's really going on.</u> Remind yourself that the turf protector is probably scared. From their point of view, you've challenged their power, their credibility, their usefulness, and possibly even their value to their organization. You've activated their Key Engagers, and the only way they know how to respond is to get in your way. They hurt, and they think *you're* the cause.

8. <u>Empathize.</u> Two sentences showing you understand are all you need. For instance, "I understand your point. I apologize if my letter has caused any problems for you. That was not the intent."

9. <u>Without pausing, reiterate your objective and offer them an option to win.</u> Explain that all you need are the answers to a few basic

questions (Did your recipient see and read your letter? Do they wish to grant your request? Did the letter get routed to someone else, and to whom?). Say that once you have these answers, your process is complete and you won't need to follow up anymore. Then—without pausing—ask, "Can you get me the answers to those questions?" If they can, wonderful; once you have them, you're done. But if they can't, say, "If you can get those answers for me, or if you can send me to someone who *can* get them for me, I'll be finished. I'll log them into our database, and I won't need to follow up anymore."

Suddenly you've given the turf protector a set of options and a way to end their contact with you and come out looking like a winner. (Remember, turf protectors need to have choices, to see an opportunity to win, and to feel like they are in supreme control.)

When the conversation is over, analyze it and assess the situation. You may want to continue prospecting the organization as usual, or follow up only with certain selected people, or stop the process. A lot depends on what responses you've already received from others, how far into the follow-up process you are, who the turf protector is (i.e., your prospect vs. a high-ranking Leverage Point vs. a stranger low in the hierarchy), and what the complaint was. Generally, though, if the turf protector did not call on someone else's behalf, I finish flushing out everyone I sent letters to in the organization.

And if the turf protector is *acting* like they've got the power to cancel a meeting you've already booked, offer to include them in the meeting. It makes them feel back in the action.

In Summary:

- Turf protectors take the C.O.L. as a personal affront and may make it their business to try to block or punish you.

- If you get a nasty letter from a turf protector, file and forget it.

- If a turf protector gets you on the phone, follow these guidelines:

    1. Be courteous, attentive, kind, and strong, no matter what they say. Just listen.

2. Let them gush.

3. Don't get defensive or begin a counterattack.

4. Qualify them by asking for their name, title, and relationship to the prospect you've targeted in their organization.

5. Ask if they're calling on their own behalf, or at the request of some other person or group. If they're not one of your prospects or Leverage Points, ask them how they found out about you.

6. Reiterate their main complaint so they know you've heard and understood them.

7. Remember what's really going on: the turf protector is scared because you've challenged their power and activated their Key Engagers.

8. Empathize for a few sentences.

9. Explain that all you need are the answers to your basic questions. Once you have these answers, your process is complete and you won't need to follow up anymore.

- When the conversation is over, analyze the conversation and assess the situation to determine whether—and whom—to keep prospecting.

Thirty-Two

Dealing with Voice Mail

In Chapter 4, I discussed how new communications technologies are making it easier and easier for your prospects to tune you out. Now I'd like to show you how to use one of these important technologies—voice mail—to your advantage.

In one very important way, voice mail has truly improved communication: It ensures that your message gets through in *exactly* the way you want it to be heard. It allows your prospect or Leverage Point to hear your voice, the intensity of your message, and its full content—not some summary that's been filtered through an assistant.

We haven't even begun to catch up to the technology, however. Most people haven't the faintest idea how to use voice mail to their advantage. They think that briefer is better, and it rarely occurs to them that "briefer" gives their listener no motivation to respond.

Here's the kind of voice mail message most people leave:

"Hi, Bob, this is Stefanie Rhinelander calling from FGH Associates at 2 P.M. on Monday, January tenth. Could you please return my call at your convenience? I'm at 910-555-5555. Thanks very much. Have a good day."

Now let me ask you a few questions.

Does anything about the message make you want to return the call?

If you were pressed for time, would you return this person's call? Case closed.

Remember, *the more your prospects and Leverage Points rely on technology to protect themselves, the more you must use that technology to remind them of the leverage you possess.* Therefore, when leaving a voice mail message, include *exactly* the same information you would if you were speaking to a secretary or assistant, and mention every bit of internal *and* external leverage you possess.

How to Leave a C.O.L. Voice Mail Message

Don't worry about how long your message takes. It may seem long at first, but your C.O.L. voice mail messages will actually be only one minute long once you've had some practice.

Your speech should be crisp, relaxed, even, and a bit slower than normal. Your tone should be cordial, not excited or schmoozy.

Do the following, more or less in order:

1. Lead with the person's first name only. "Hi, Eli . . ."

2. State your name, your title or level of responsibility ("I run the Portland office of . . ."), and the organization you represent, if any.

3. Announce the day and the time of your call.

4. State your relationship to the person, if you have one ("I'm calling at the request of . . ." "I was referred to you by . . ."). If you have no relationship, then say so ("I have no credibility with you, and you don't know me, but . . .").

5. Mention your letter, when it was sent, when it should have been received, and the names and titles of everyone else in the organization who was sent a copy.

6. Explain that you're calling to find out if they received and read your letter, and if they are interested in granting the access it requested.

7. Quickly and clearly state the key benefits of your offer and/ or your key point(s) of difference. If appropriate, add your positioning statement.

8. Mention whatever external leverage you can ("Our customers include . . ." "Later this week I'll be meeting with your counterpart, Kaia Olsen, at OPQ International . . .").

9. Ask for a response, and provide guidelines on how to reach you ("I'm usually in the office from 9 until 11 A.M."). If you have an 800 number and/or a secretary, say so. If your name is difficult to spell or pronounce, repeat it and spell it. I almost always add, "I don't need to speak to you. I'd just like to know if you saw my letter, and if you wish to grant my request."

10. Explain that you will follow up again in two or three days if you've not gotten a response. If this is your second message to the person and they have not returned the first one, add, "I'll keep following up until I get your response." Watch how fast you get a response!

11. As a final reminder of the leverage you've created, mention that you'll be following up with the other recipients of your letter, to learn of their responses.

12. Thank your listener and end the call.

For Advanced Players Only

In Chapter 24 I explained how to make initial contact with your prospects and Leverage Points by letter. Under certain conditions, though, it may make sense to make your first contact by phone. These conditions are

Sample Initial Voice Mail Message To Prospect

ESSENTIAL ELEVEN QUESTIONS		WHY IS THIS NECESSARY?
Who are you? What do you do?	This is _____. I run the _____ department at _____. I'm calling Tuesday the ninth at 4 P.M.	To position yourself as credible.
Why are you calling me? Who else do you do this for?	We've never met, and I don't have any connection or credibility with you. However, I'm calling because next week I expect to be meeting with individuals at your level at several other major companies in your business when I'm in town, and I thought it would be smart to see you as well. *(If you have at least one* *appointment scheduled with* *a competing company,* *mention them here, including* *the names of your prospects* *and their companies.)*	The listener is trying to recall if they have met you or talked with you. You're helping them by quickly answering what they want to know, when they want to know it. You're also applying the leverage of their key competitors.
What's this about?	We help people in your business to [key benefits one, two, and three]. Our key points of difference are _____ and _____. We may be able to do the same for you, once I understand your specific needs.	Get to the point. The listener now knows the basics. You're championing the needs of their organization.

What do you want from me? Who else are you sending this message to?	I'm calling to find out who is the most appropriate person to meet with. I'm also putting in calls today to [names of Leverage Points within the listener's organization] to leave this very same message.	Draws a circle of leverage around the listener.
What do you want from me? How long will it take?	I'd like to schedule a twenty-minute meeting with you, or whoever is the appropriate person, regarding [your offer].	This brief time period makes it easy for your listener to say yes to your request.
When do you want it?	We can meet at _____ on the afternoon of _____ or _____ .	Continues to fill in the listener's picture.
Who needs to be involved?	Most of the customers we deal with involve their CFOs, vice presidents of _____, and _____s because _____. Therefore, you may wish to include them as you see fit.	
Who else do you do this for? How will it benefit my organization?	As we are doing for [names of some of recipient's major competitors], once I understand your specific needs, there is a good chance that we can help you via the [key benefits] we deliver.	Continues to keep their Key Engagers activated.

I will be following up with
your assistant within the next
few days. Please let them
know if you wish to meet,
and what dates and times
will work for you.

I can be reached at [phone
number]. If you get my
secretary, please let her
know what times would
work.

Mentioning that
you have a
secretary may
boost your
credibility.

I look forward to meeting
with you. Thank you very
much. I'll be listening for
your response.

- You have used the C.O.L. in a minimum of ten prospecting situations, feel comfortable with it, and have become fluent in using it.

- You have excellent telephone skills and a good phone manner.

- You are in an urgent prospecting situation—e.g., you need access very quickly, or you're first approaching your prospect very late in the decision-making process.

On pages 260–262 is a sample voice mail message that makes a first contact with a prospect or Leverage Point. With some modifications, this message also works well for talking with live people.

This message answers all the Essential Eleven questions (see page 193) that any good C.O.L. letter must address. Each question appears in the left-hand column; the part of the message that addresses the question appears immediately to its right.

In Summary:

- The more your prospects and Leverage Points rely on technology to protect themselves, the more you can use that technology to remind them of the leverage you possess.

- When leaving a voice mail message, include exactly the same information you would if you were speaking to a secretary, and mention every bit of internal and external leverage you possess.

- Under certain conditions you may want to make your initial contact with prospects and Leverage Points by phone.

- Any such phone message should answer the same Essential Eleven questions that any good C.O.L. letter addresses.

Thirty-Three

You're In! Now What?

Staying Alert

You're feeling good. Your prospect has officially scheduled the meeting or conference you requested. The C.O.L. did its job.

That's the good news. But here's some additional news.

Once your appointment has been granted and booked, one of a hundred things can suddenly arise to take it away. Some of these—illness, disaster, emergency—you can't do anything about. (In these cases, prospects are usually willing to reschedule.)

But you need to be aware of a much more insidious—and common—problem: the continued huffing and puffing of turf protectors.

As you use the C.O.L. successfully, sooner or later you're going to discover a message like this on your voice mail:

"This is Ben Short. I'm the Associate Director of Purchasing here at UVW Manufacturing. I'm calling on behalf of my boss, Nancy Tur-abian, in regard to the letter you sent her about your services. I know you're scheduled to meet with her on the nineteenth; however, she's given me your letter and asked me to call you. I have a few questions I'd like to get answered to determine if there really is a need to meet, so please call me at your earliest convenience at 801-555-5555 so we can talk further."

This kind of message can appear out of nowhere, and it can come in many different forms. But regardless of where it comes from or what form it's in, it usually means someone is trying to scuttle your plans.

Occasionally a message such as this means exactly what it says: Your prospect is having second thoughts or a change of heart. But the vast majority of the time, that's not what's happening at all.

What's really going on is this: The turf protectors, the underlings, the defensive guards who are supposed to be protecting their king or queen, have finally become aware of who you are. They're bothered that you've somehow slipped past them and gotten around or through their steel barricades—all without causing any commotion, and with-out their knowledge. You're about to have an audience with their sovereign leader, and they've been completely cut out of the loop!

As you can imagine, you've activated every one of their Key En-gagers big time. Their emotions are flying all over the place. They're asking themselves rapid-fire questions and trying to puff themselves up:

What's this all about?

Why wasn't I informed?

I should probably handle this, shouldn't I?

Why does this person need to meet with my boss?

I'm supposed to be taking care of things like this! Why didn't this person call me?

Oh, God, maybe I wasn't doing my job. I hope I don't look stupid.

This sounds like what we already have (or what we're already looking at), only repackaged, so I'll save my boss some time, stress, and hassle. Besides, my boss doesn't need to spend time on this matter. I'll call this person and say, "No thanks, we don't need what you've got." I'll be a hero!

In short, their power base is threatened. They're scared, and they're fighting back. And the best way for them to feel important, powerful, and secure once again is for them to somehow shoot you down.

This is why you must always be prepared to use your leverage at all times—up until the very moment when your meeting or conference begins.

If you find yourself in this situation, don't panic. You can regain the upper hand by doing the following:

1. Refuse to take the turf protector's threat terribly seriously. Remember, they're doing their best to trip *your* Key Engagers. The more upset or anxious you become, the more powerful they will feel—and the more they will try to shut you out. So throughout your dealings, remain calm and unruffled. Don't forget, you're still playing a game.

2. Nevertheless, do respond to them by phone—and in your call, *bury* them in leverage. It doesn't matter whether you speak to them directly, or to their assistant, or to their voice mail—but inform them of every bit of leverage you've created. For example:

"Thanks for your call. I understand you've got some concerns about the meeting Martin Sprung has scheduled with me. That's a decision he made based on a letter I sent him on June twenty-eighth. Maybe you've seen it, because copies also went out to your Vice President of Finance, your CFO, and your COO. Since that letter was sent, I've been in touch with the offices of all three of those individuals, as well as your boss. The meeting concerns a software product my company has sold to many Fortune 500 firms, including several of your direct competitors. In fact, in the next few weeks I'll be meeting with key executives at some of your direct competitors, including _____, _____, and _____."

3. Invite them to the meeting! The reason they're so bothered is they've been cut out of the loop—so you may utterly disarm them by asking them to join you. For example: "I think it would be a good idea if you were there as well. Is that possible?"

4. Now get off the phone as quickly as possible. The longer you stay on, the more opportunities the turf protector has to try to erode your leverage by drawing you into your presentation.

If they start asking questions about your offer, don't allow yourself to be talked into making your presentation on the phone. *Briefly* run through the main benefits of your offer, your key points of difference, and, if appropriate, your positioning statement. Then bring the conversation to a close: "So when you and your boss meet with me on _____, what you'll get in _____ minutes is a detailed presentation on _____, _____, and _____. I look forward to meeting you and _____(boss's first name) in person on _____ at _____."

Never, never send turf protectors any additional information by mail, even if they request it, because they'll very likely use it as a way to freeze you out. They may look it over, then call back again and say, "Thanks for the information. We've examined it carefully, and if we have a need for your product we'll certainly get back to you, but based on what you've sent us, there's no need to meet at this point." End of discussion—and end of appointment.

And *absolutely do not* try to convince turf protectors of the benefits they or their boss will gain by granting you access. That plays right into their hands. Remember, you've *already got* the access you need. If you try to talk your way in once again, you're sunk, because you've acted as if your appointment isn't a done deal, which it is—and you've let the turf protector put themselves into a one-up position. Just get off the phone!

If a turf protector starts making noises about canceling your appointment, or about having to reconsider or regrant the meeting (even though you know it's still scheduled), call their bluff, then remind them of your leverage yet again. "Since your boss scheduled the meeting with the blessing of your COO, CFO, and Vice President of Finance, I presume all of them think it's a good idea. Of course, if your boss does decide he needs to cancel, I'm sure he'll have his secretary call to let me know."

Bad News Isn't Always Bad News

Now let's look at the worst-case scenario: You get a call from a turf protector telling you that your meeting with their boss has been canceled. Don't take this lying down. *Immediately* call your prospect (*not* the turf protector) and leave a message to this effect with their secretary or on their voice mail:

"Henry, I've just received a call from Adrienne Kreger, who has informed me that the meeting we've scheduled on May first has been canceled. Since the meeting was scheduled through your office, and since I've been in touch with _____, _____, and _____ [Henry's internal leverage points], my understanding was that the meeting was scheduled at their request and approval. Please have your assistant return my call to let me know whether the meeting is still on as planned or whether it has indeed been canceled. If we need to reschedule for another day or time, I'm happy to do that. I can be reached at 515-555-5555."

Believe it or not, you'll find that half the time your meeting wasn't canceled at all! Your pal the turf protector was simply flexing their muscles and taking a shot at getting rid of you. They might even have told their boss that *you* canceled the meeting. By being strong and direct, and not acknowledging what power, if any, the turf protector might have, you keep them honest and accountable.

If it turns out that your meeting actually *has* been canceled, you'll have to make your best seat-of-the-pants judgment whether to apply additional leverage on your prospect, try to gain access with someone else in the organization, or move on.

Incidentally, if your prospect merely *postpones* a meeting to another specific date and time, of course be gracious about it. It's highly unlikely that they're trying to blow you off. *Do*, however, resist any attempts to postpone an appointment to some unspecified time, such as "later in the month" or "next week." That gives your prospect the chance to shut you out by simply not responding. Push hard to schedule a specific date and time, and try to offer a wide range of possibilities.

A Word About Confirming Appointments

***Don't*. I repeat: *Never* confirm any appointment, no matter who it's with or where it is.** Don't confirm it by phone, by fax, by letter, by E-mail, or by carrier pigeon. Just show up!

I know this is the exact opposite of what we've all been taught, especially if you must travel a good distance for the appointment. However, any time you confirm an appointment, you give your prospect a great opportunity to reconsider whether they really want to see you. *Never* give them this opportunity.

When you simply show up, the meeting will almost always take place as planned. While you run a small risk that the meeting may get lost or forgotten in the daily shuffle, calling to confirm creates a much bigger risk of being shut out entirely.

In the very remote chance that your prospect has truly forgotten, they will probably feel bad and reschedule immediately. And guess what? That gives you a bit more leverage when you do meet.

In Summary:

- Be prepared to use your leverage at all times, up until the very moment your meeting or conference begins.

- If you get a call from a turf protector who acts as if they have the power to regrant or cancel an appointment you've already scheduled, do the following:

  *Refuse to take their threat seriously.

  *Repeat every bit of leverage you've created.

  *Invite them to your meeting or conference.

  *Get off the phone as quickly as possible.

  *If they start asking questions about your offer, don't let them pull you into your presentation. Run through the main benefits of your offer, your key points of difference, and, if appropriate, your positioning statement. Then bring the conversation to a close.

- Never send turf protectors any additional information by mail, even if requested.

- Never try to convince a turf protector of the benefits of granting you access. This plays right into their hands.

- If you get a call from a turf protector telling you that your meeting with their boss has been canceled, *immediately* check this out with the boss (or their assistant).

- *Never* confirm *any* appointment—just show up. Most people remember and honor scheduled appointments.

MASTERING THE CIRCLE
OF LEVERAGE SYSTEM

Thirty-Four

Sample Scenarios and Case Histories

The stories that follow are actual accounts of the Circle of Leverage System in action. Both of these scenarios took place in 1995.

Scenario #1

It's fitting to begin with the story of how I secured a publishing contract for this book from one of the largest book publishers in the country.

Not knowing anything about the publishing business, I began to study the industry. I had the research director of the Minneapolis Public Library gather information for me, and I talked to bookstore owners, authors, and agents. Here is what I learned:

The book publishing business is a very closed industry. It is normally very difficult to get in the door for a face-to-face appointment—especially for someone like me, a first-time author with no credibility, no publications, no other track record, and no connections to rely on.

The ten biggest book publishers receive between 2,500 and 5,000 book proposals *every month*. So I knew the odds of getting my book published by a major publishing house were extremely slim.

Standard operating procedure among publishers is *not* to meet with authors but to review book proposals sent to them by agents. Then, if they are impressed by a proposal, they sometimes talk or meet with the author. Normally, though, they deal only with agents.

With this as background, I began to build an appropriate "get in the door" strategy. I made a couple of key decisions, both of which went completely against the grain of how things worked (and still do work) in the industry.

First, I decided that I would *not* have my agent send out my book proposal in the usual way. (This would be like sending out all my information right away—giving my prospects no incentive to meet with me.) Instead, I would try to book in-person appointments first. At each appointment I would make an in-person presentation, then leave the proposal behind. By insisting on meeting with editors and publishers in person first, I would also demonstrate exactly how the C.O.L. worked. (Remember what I said about controlling the information flow?)

This turned out to be a key decision. I needed something to make me stand out, some key point of difference. This was it.

Second, instead of having my agent do all the usual canvassing and qualifying, I chose to be the front man. My agent agreed to stay in the background until I arrived in New York for the appointments I would schedule with editors and publishers.

Here is what I did:

• Preparation Step #1: I decided that what I needed was a thirty-minute in-person presentation at each publishing house.

• Preparation Step #2: After doing some initial research, I chose to target eleven of the largest and best-known consumer-oriented book publishers in the nation, which were all based in New York. I pulled executive profile information on these publishers, as well as detailed lists of staff. I verified every person's name, title, phone number, and fax number through calls to the publishers' switchboards.

• Preparation Step #3: Knowing full well that in publishers' eyes I was a rookie with no track record or credibility whatsoever, I realized I needed to create a great deal of leverage. After consulting with my literary agent about the level of individuals who had the power to say yes, I decided that I would be satisfied if I could get face-to-face meetings at four or five companies, with either the publisher, the editorial director of adult trade (i.e., consumer) books, or an editor who specialized in self-help or business books. I also wanted to get sales and marketing vice presidents in these meetings.

I decided on three to seven key people per publisher who would receive my letter simultaneously. (Letters ultimately landed on close to sixty people's desks on the same day.) I was aware that many of these people know one another well, so I was confident that each company would provide a good deal of leverage against the others.

• Preparation Step #4: From further research, and from talking with my agent, I learned more about the characteristics and atmosphere of the publishing business.

• Preparation Step #5: In crystallizing the benefits of my offer, I was able to point to several things: the timeliness of my book; its uniqueness; its wide application and audience; and the desperate need for a solution to the problem of access that millions of people deal with day after day. I was also able to provide endorsements from about a dozen influential people, which I had gathered over the previous months, as well as a foreword by David McNally, which I had just commissioned.

• Preparation Step #6: Using research from the Minneapolis Public Library, I identified and studied all the books that publishers might view as competitive with mine. I learned that there existed only a handful of books on the topic of getting in. I specifically positioned my book against all of these—as the first and only step-by-step system to help anyone get in their desired prospects' doors. I also developed a promotion and marketing plan for my book based on what Harvey Mackay, one of the country's most successful nonfiction authors, had done for his own first book, *Swim With the Sharks*.

• Preparation Step #7: I did some soul-searching and understood that I deserved to get in because of the power and value of my system, the quality of my book proposal, the strength of the in-person presentation I had prepared, and my willingness to fly to New York to meet with editors and publishers.

275

• Preparation Step #8: Because I had a plan similar to Harvey Mackay's, an introduction from David McNally, significant endorsements, and a strong position against the competition, I was able to create just enough concern and curiosity among editors and publishers that if they didn't grant me access, they might miss an opportunity to sell lots of books.

• Preparation Step #9: I assessed my firepower and admitted I had only a small amount at best—the endorsements, the David McNally introduction, and an agent who believed in the book.

• Preparation Step #10: I reviewed my mind-set and passed my own pest test.

• Execution Steps: I prepared my C.O.L. letter in consultation with my agent (who advised me on industry terminology) and sent letters to all targeted individuals at all eleven publishers on the same day, by Federal Express. Two days later I began my follow-up calls to flush out my prospects.

You already know the outcome, of course. St. Martin's Press made an offer of publication, which I accepted. But let me fill you in with a few details.

Of the eleven publishers I approached, *all* of them responded to my letter within three business days. Five granted face-to-face, thirty-minute meetings. (One of these had to be postponed when the editorial director fell ill; ultimately, I chose not to take the meeting.) Each meeting was with either an editorial vice president, publisher, editorial director, editor-in-chief, editor, or some combination. At one publishing company, a marketing director sat in as well.

Now let me tell you one revealing anecdote. At one of the largest publishers I had targeted, I sent letters to the CEO, the Senior Vice President of Sales and Marketing, the Publisher of Adult Trade Books, two Associate Publishers, and the Vice President of Sales. As I began flushing out my prospect, I was told politely but firmly by the assistants of two executives, "This really doesn't sound like our type of book, so there's no point in scheduling a meeting."

You might think the prospects for an appointment with this company weren't very bright. But I've had enough experience with the C.O.L. to know that the show wasn't over.

A day or two later I got a call from the office of the Vice President and Publisher of the company's business line—someone I had not targeted at all. "Our Publisher would like to meet with you when you're in New York," the Publisher's assistant told me.

It turned out that two of my letters had been routed to him, and he was very intrigued. I booked the appointment.

This happens all the time. The power struggles in major corporations are sometimes immense, and you never know people's real agendas. So remember, when someone says, "No thanks," half the time the show is not over.

Scenario #2

I had just created a three-day training product, The Power to Get In Seminar and Workshop, and was ready to sell it. Because this was a brand-new product, I hadn't trained anyone yet. I knew that many of my prospects would perceive me as just another one of the hundreds of sales trainers unless I could clearly position myself against everyone else.

Although I had decided early on to target the insurance industry, I was very aware that this industry is heavily prospected by sales training companies. I knew it would be difficult to stand out and be noticed. Again, I had no credibility, track record, or referrals.

I chose to target ten of the biggest and best-known insurance companies in the nation. Here's what I did:

• Preparation Step #1: I decided that what I really needed was a thirty-minute in-person appointment where I could present the benefits of the unique workshop I had created. I also decided it was worth the expense to fly to each company's headquarters in order to make my presentation, if I could get the right decision makers in the room.

• Preparation Step #2: After researching the industry and many potential companies, I chose to target some of the largest publicly held insurance firms in the New York/New Jersey metro area. Using information from *The Yellow Book*, I put together my Organization Profiles and pinpointed my prospects and Leverage Points.

• Preparation Step #3: I chose as my prospects the senior vice presidents of field sales. I selected three Leverage Points for each prospect; depending on the firm, these included the presidents, CEOs, CFOs, and/or senior vice presidents of agency operations or marketing. Since all the companies were in direct competition with one another, I knew that each person who received my letter would be a Leverage Point for virtually everyone else.

• Preparation Step #4: In researching the industry, I learned that my prospects were 75 percent men, ages forty to fifty-five, with incomes over $250,000. I also knew, from both experience and the grapevine, that these people tended to be precise, organized time misers who had very sharp assistants.

• Preparation Step #5: I crystallized the net benefits of my workshop into a single concise statement: "The Power to Get In Seminar and Workshop help people get access to their prospects faster, more effectively, and with less expense."

• Preparation Step #6: My key point of difference was that I was not a sales training company, not a presentation skills trainer, not a marketing consultant, and not a "how to close a deal" specialist. I was strictly a "get in the door" expert. My positioning statement became: *Helping people get in.*™

• Preparation Step #7: I knew I deserved to get in because I had something truly different, something my prospects genuinely needed—and something no one else could offer.

• Preparation Step #8: One benefit of granting me access was finding out about something truly new, different, and state-of-the-art. And because I had targeted all ten companies at once—and everyone receiving my letter knew it—another benefit of granting me access was keeping up with the competition.

• Preparation Step #9: I took stock of my firepower and knew I had nothing beyond whatever leverage I could generate. This was sobering knowledge, but it helped me stay grounded.

• Preparation Step #10: I knew my research was solid and my in-person presentation was crisp and convincing. I was confident and secure in what I was offering. I passed my pest test with honors.

• Execution Steps: I wrote a one-page C.O.L. letter, which I sent by regular mail. Five days after the letters hit the mail, I made my follow-up calls to flush out my prospects.

The results? I got the exact meetings I wanted with the exact people I wanted in five out of the ten companies—a 50 percent success rate.

Let me tell you exactly how I got in at one company that employs more than five thousand agents in the United States alone.

The CEO of the company read my letter and threw it away. The

Senior Vice President of Field Sales skimmed my letter and trashed it as well. The Senior Vice President of Marketing never saw his letter at all because his assistant routed it to the Director of Training.

When I called the CFO's assistant, I learned that he had routed my letter *up*, to the CEO. The CEO (who had thrown out his own letter) now reread the letter and placed a call to the Senior Vice President of Field Sales (who also had thrown away his copy of the letter). In essence, the CEO said, "Maybe he has something for us. He's meeting with some of our direct competition, and he's only asking for a thirty-minute appointment. Maybe we should check this out." The Senior Vice President of Field Sales then routed the CEO's message down to one of his direct reports, the Vice President and Director of Agency Operations, directing him to call me and set up an appointment.

Two weeks later I was in front of the person who had full power to purchase my workshop—for a group of five thousand end users. I was in front of the correct decision makers on the first call.

Now, do you think most sales training companies selling to the insurance industry start out by meeting with the Vice President and Director of Agency Operations? Hardly. It's more likely they start with the Manager of Training at a branch or regional office. Three, five, or seven meetings later, they'd normally arrive where I was already—*if* they and their prospect did everything right.

That's how powerful the C.O.L. is.

Thirty-Five

Exercises for Practicing the Circle of Leverage System

The best way to become proficient in the C.O.L. is to practice it. You can't expect to master it right away. Becoming skilled takes time and practice. This final chapter provides you with three opportunities to carry out the entire C.O.L., step by step.

To get the maximum benefit from this chapter, I urge you to treat each prospecting situation as if it were real: Do the appropriate research, complete all the necessary forms, and write a strong C.O.L. letter that will activate your prospects' and Leverage Points' Key Engagers. If you like, imagine or role-play your follow-up calls.

Copies of all the forms and charts used elsewhere in this book appear on the following pages.

At the end of this chapter are two extremely useful supplements. The first is a three-page C.O.L. Inventory, which presents the highlights of each step and an overview of each prospecting situation. It's designed so you can use it as your road map each time. Use it to plan out and execute each "get in the door" strategy. The inventory is a place to record key information from many of the forms on the following pages. Properly filled in, this inventory will enable you to assess your circumstances and strategy at a glance.

The second supplement is a basic template that will help you design a strong Circle of Leverage letter for any situation.

Situation #1

You're a small business owner who has just started your own software development company. Your specialty is custom-developing software applications for businesses of all sizes. You have ten years of experience in software design, development, and implementation, which you've gained through working for three other software development firms. Your company has two employees: you and your secretary.

You've decided to call on businesses with fifty or more employees that you think might need custom software development or redesign. You need to get in the doors of these companies to explain the benefits of your services.

Situation #2

After a successful career as a marketing assistant at one of the divisions of AT&T, you learn that you (and 20,000 others) are about to be displaced by a massive downsizing and reorganizing effort.

Over the past five years, you've developed and demonstrated good marketing and communication skills. You have some brochure-design experience, and you've written ad copy for a variety of services and products, from small business services to mobile communications.

You're looking for a new job—and you're one of (probably) hundreds of people in your city with similar skills and backgrounds.

Situation #3

You're twenty-five years old. Three years ago you graduated from the University of Oregon with a bachelor's degree in communications. Since then, you haven't been able to find satisfactory employment. You've chosen to spend the last two and a half years working through temporary agencies, and as a result have gained a great deal of office management experience, working in more than twenty companies.

You decide you would like a job as a full-time office manager or executive secretary. The size of the company and the field don't matter.

You've already decided that responding to help wanted ads and sending your résumé to human resources offices won't get you anywhere.

Organization Profile

Name _____

Branches, units, divisions, subsidiaries _____

_____

_____

_____

_____

Address (main headquarters) _____

Main phone (headquarters) _____

Main fax (headquarters) _____

Address (specific division or unit) _____

Main phone (division or unit) _____

Main fax (division or unit) _____

Web site address _____

Number of employees: entire organization _____

                      division or unit _____

Primary business(es) _____

_____

Secondary business(es) _____

_____

Profit (or loss): last year _____

      19_____   _____

      19_____   _____

      19_____   _____

      19_____   _____

Board of directors (names)   Chair: _____

_____

_____

_____

_____

_____

_____

Officers of the corporation

     Title _____   Name _____

     Title _____   Name _____

     Title _____   Name _____

     Title _____   Name _____

     Title _____   Name _____

     Title _____   Name _____

Key executives and their assistants

1. Title _____   Name _____

     Address _____

     Phone _____   Fax _____

     Assistant's name _____

     Phone _____   Fax _____

2. Title _____   Name _____

     Address _____

     Phone _____   Fax _____

     Assistant's name _____

     Phone _____   Fax _____

3. Title _____   Name _____

     Address _____

     Phone _____   Fax _____

     Assistant's name _____

     Phone _____   Fax _____

4. Title _____   Name _____

     Address _____

     Phone _____   Fax _____

     Assistant's name _____

     Phone _____   Fax _____

5. Title _____   Name _____

     Address _____

     Phone _____   Fax _____

     Assistant's name _____

     Phone _____   Fax _____

6. Title _____   Name _____

     Address _____

     Phone _____   Fax _____

     Assistant's name _____

     Phone _____   Fax _____

7. Title _____ Name _____
    Address _____
    Phone _____ Fax _____
    Assistant's name _____
    Phone _____ Fax _____

Other important people and their assistants

8. Title _____ Name _____
    Address _____
    Phone _____ Fax _____
    Assistant's name _____
    Phone _____ Fax _____

9. Title _____ Name _____
    Address _____
    Phone _____ Fax _____
    Assistant's name _____
    Phone _____ Fax _____

10. Title _____ Name _____
    Address _____
    Phone _____ Fax _____
    Assistant's name _____
    Phone _____ Fax _____

11. Title _____ Name _____
    Address _____
    Phone _____ Fax _____
    Assistant's name _____
    Phone _____ Fax _____

Significant corporate events _____
_____
_____

Other information _____
_____
_____
_____
_____
_____
_____

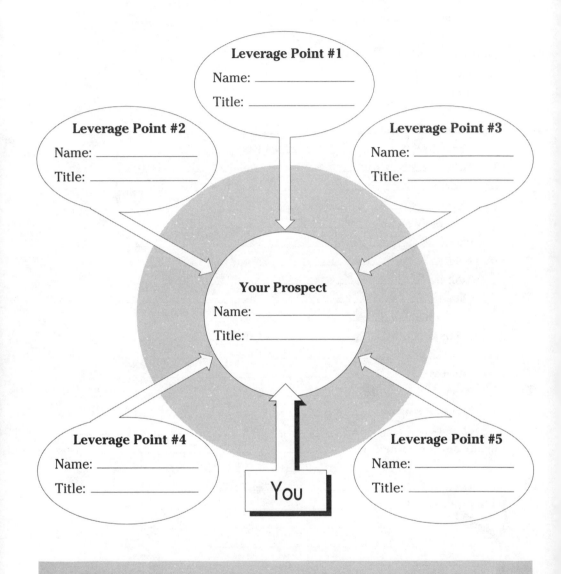

The Leverage You Have Created Gets You in the Door

Prospect Portrait

Name _____ Title _____

Company _____

Division/unit/subsidiary _____

Job description/duties _____

_____

Address _____

Phone _____ Fax _____

E-mail _____ Web site _____

Name/title of prospect's superior _____

Assistant's name _____ Phone _____

Fax _____ E-mail _____

Prospect's sex ___ Age ___ Marital status ___ Annual salary _____

Amount of power within organization/division _____

Number of years in organization _____ in position _____

Prior position and company _____

General temperament _____

What motivates them? _____

_____

What's important to them? _____

_____

Character traits that may help me get in _____

_____

Character traits that may hinder my getting in _____

_____

Other relevant information _____

_____

Competition Profile

Competitor #1 (name) _____

Benefit #1 _____

Benefit #2 _____

Benefit #3 _____

Positioning statement/slogan _____

Competitor #2 (name) _____

Benefit #1 _____

Benefit #2 _____

Benefit #3 _____

Positioning statement/slogan _____

Competitor #3 (name) _____

Benefit #1 _____

Benefit #2 _____

Benefit #3 _____

Positioning statement/slogan _____

Competitor #4 (name) _____

Benefit #1 _____

Benefit #2 _____

Benefit #3 _____

Positioning statement/slogan _____

Competitor #5 (name) _____

Benefit #1 _____

Benefit #2 _____

Benefit #3 _____

Positioning statement/slogan _____

Positioning Worksheet

The key benefits of my offer are:

Benefit #1 _____

Benefit #2 _____

Benefit #3 _____

Therefore, my offer's key points of difference are:

#1 _____

#2 _____

#3 _____

My positioning statement is:

_____

_____

Circle of Leverage Inventory

Preparation Step #1: DEFINE WHAT YOU NEED VS. WHAT YOU WANT

_____

_____

_____

_____

Preparation Step #2: DO YOUR HOMEWORK: USE THE LEVERAGE OF RE-SEARCH

Get the basic information on each prospecting situation. Complete an Organization Profile for each targeted organization.

Preparation Step #3: DECIDE WHO TO TARGET

My prospect is: _____

Leverage Point 1: _____

Leverage Point 2: _____

Leverage Point 3: _____

Leverage Point 4: _____

Leverage Point 5: _____

Direct competitors (external Leverage Points): _____

_____

_____

_____

_____

Preparation Step #4: UNDERSTAND YOUR PROSPECT'S NATURE

Fill out a Prospect Portrait for each prospect.

Name: _____ Title: _____

Company: _____ Division/unit: _____

Job description: _____

Address: _____

Phone _____ Fax: _____ E-mail: _____

Assistant's name/phone/fax: _____

What is important to your prospect? _____

What motivates them? _____

Character traits: _____

Preparation Step #5: CRYSTALLIZE THE NET BENEFITS OF YOUR OFFER
These must be demonstrable, and must be presented in sound bites.
Benefit 1: _____
Benefit 2: _____
Benefit 3: _____

Preparation Step #6: KNOW YOUR COMPETITORS' NET BENEFITS AND YOUR KEY POINTS OF DIFFERENCE—THEN ESTABLISH YOUR POSITION
Competitor 1   Name: _____
Benefit 1: _____
Benefit 2: _____
Benefit 3: _____

Competitor 2   Name: _____
Benefit 1: _____
Benefit 2: _____
Benefit 3: _____

Competitor 3   Name: _____
Benefit 1: _____
Benefit 2: _____
Benefit 3: _____

Therefore, my offer's key points of difference are:
   1. _____
   2. _____
   3. _____
My positioning statement is: _____

Preparation Step #7: WHY DO I DESERVE TO GET IN?
   Answer: _____
   _____

Preparation Step #8: CRYSTALLIZE THE NET BENEFITS OF GRANTING YOU ACCESS
   How does my prospect benefit, even if they don't accept my offer?
   _____
   _____

Preparation Step #9: TAKE STOCK OF YOUR FIREPOWER

Use your biggest guns first.

The firepower I will use includes:

_____

_____

_____

Preparation Step #10: CHECK YOUR ATTITUDE

Take the pest test.

Execution Step #1: PREPARE YOUR INITIAL COMMUNICATION AND PUT IT IN PLAY

Draft your C.O.L. letter. Include answers to the Essential Eleven questions. Your prospect and all internal Leverage Points must receive your letter simultaneously.

Execution Step #2: FLUSH OUT YOUR PROSPECT

Allow one to two business days of percolation time before you begin your phone follow-ups. Make your calls as close to simultaneously as possible. Proceed from the highest- to the lowest-ranking person in the organization. Save your prospect for last. In each call, ask:

1. Did the person receive and read your letter?
2. Do they wish to grant your request for access?
3. Did they route your letter to someone else? To whom?

Execution Step #3: DANCE, SPONGE, AND REITERATE

Mirror your prospect's or Leverage Point's behavior. Search for their biggest needs and goals. Reiterate their messages and ask for details.

Execution Step #4: ALIGN AND CHAMPION YOUR OFFER

Align your offer with the goals and mission of your prospect's organization.

Execution Step #5: OPEN THEIR DOOR

Stop pitching and ask for access. Once you're in, never confirm—just show up.

Circle of Leverage Form Letter Example

Date

Name
Title
Company
Address

Dear _____:

As _____ of _____, Inc., I am writing to you,
_____, _____, and _____ to find out who is the
most appropriate person to deal with regarding scheduling
a _____-minute in-person appointment/conference call/
video conference on (date), when I'm in town meeting with
_____, _____, and _____ (names of people)
at _____, _____, and _____ (names of companies).

Our business is helping _____. The net benefits we deliver
are _____, _____, and _____. Our customers are
_____, _____, and _____. Our key point of
difference is _____, and we are proud of our position as
the _____ of _____.

If you grant the appointment, what I will present are
_____, _____, and _____. When I follow up with
your assistant in the next few days, please let them know if
you wish to schedule the _____, and what times are good
for you. Otherwise, please direct me to whomever you wish
me to deal with regarding my request.

Thank you. I look forward to meeting with you.

Sincerely,

Name

Some Final Words
of Encouragement

I want to thank you for the time you've invested in reading this book. I feel particularly fortunate to have collected about fifteen years of excellent street experience in the art of getting in, all of which helped me create the system I have shared with you.

Like anything of value in life, the C.O.L. takes practice before you become proficient at it. Expect mistakes—they're the only way you'll learn. I wish my own execution of the System were perfect every time, but I still make mistakes myself.

Never forget that getting in the door is an art form. Don't expect to become a Picasso overnight. Be patient with yourself and with the C.O.L. You must trust it, even if at first you don't believe it will work for you.

Much success to you!

—*Michael A. Boylan*

About the Creator of the
Circle of Leverage™ System

Michael A. Boylan is founder and CEO of The Boylan Group, Incorporated, a company dedicated to helping people of all professions and backgrounds get in the door of their desired prospects faster, more effectively, and with less expense, so they can increase their income and achieve better overall results.

Mr. Boylan has developed and used the Circle of Leverage™ System to get meetings, phone consultations, or other access to the presidents and senior executives of many of this country's largest corporations, including General Motors, AT&T, ITT, Prudential, RJR Nabisco, American Express, Citicorp, Johnson & Johnson, PaineWebber, SmithKline Beecham, Time Warner, Pfizer, RCA, MCA, Bertelsmann Music Group, Amway Corporation, The Equitable, The Travelers, Chase Manhattan Bank, Chemical Bank, Tenneco Oil, Dayton-Hudson, Household Finance International, Shell Oil, BASF Corporation, Conoco Oil, USX Corporation, and many others.

Prior to founding The Boylan Group, Mr. Boylan founded and built Automated Telemarketing Services, a highly successful company marketing Predictive Dialing Systems and Call Processing Networks throughout the U.S., Canada, and the United Kingdom, serving large and small companies in the retail, credit card processing, telemarketing, and collections industries. ATS's customers include Household Finance International, Banc One, Harris Bank, Fingerhut, Citicorp, and many others. He also co-founded Verifications, Inc., which provides background credential verification services to the HR departments of large and small corporations.

The Circle of Leverage™ System has been instrumental in helping Mr. Boylan get in the door, then close a variety of multimillion-dollar sales to corporations in the retail, banking, telemarketing, and collections industries. None of these sales would have been as fast or as efficient—or even possible at all—without the Circle of Leverage™ System.

Currently, Mr. Boylan consults, lectures, and leads training sessions on the Circle of Leverage™ System for organizations of all types and sizes, as well as for business owners, senior executives, mid-level managers, and sales and marketing professionals. He lives in suburban Minneapolis.

About the Boylan Group, Incorporated

The Boylan Group, Inc. exists to help people of all professions, backgrounds, and skill levels to get in the doors of their desired prospects—whoever they may be—faster, more effectively, and with less expense, so they can increase their incomes and achieve greater results.

We help:

- Business people: top executives, business owners, managers, and sales and marketing professionals of companies of all sizes

- People in job and career transitions—and people who wish to enter or reenter the work force

- Recent and soon-to-be college graduates

We offer the following products and services:

- The Power to Get In™ Seminar and Workshop for companies of all sizes

- The Power to Get In™ One-Day Seminar for both companies and individuals (delivered both in-house and as a public seminar)

- The Power to Get In™ Cassette Home Study Course

- Custom consulting and speaking

If you'd like more information on any of the above products or services, please write, fax, or call:

The Boylan Group, Incorporated
9941 Deerbrook Drive
Suite 100
Minneapolis, MN 55317
Phone: (612) 445-1012
Fax: (612) 445-5015